Fundamentals of

Menu Planning

DISCARDED

DISCARDED

Fundamentals of
Menu Planning

Second Edition

Paul J. McVety

Bradley J. Ware

Claudette Lévesque

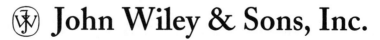 John Wiley & Sons, Inc.

New York   Chichester   Weinheim   Brisbane   Singapore   Toronto

Diane M. Halle Library
ENDICOTT COLLEGE
Beverly, MA 01915

This book is printed on acid-free paper. ∞

Copyright © 2001 by John Wiley & Sons. All rights reserved.

Published simultaneously in Canada.

No part of this publication may be reproduced, stored in a retrieval system or transmitted in any form or by any means, electronic, mechanical, photocopying, recording, scanning or otherwise, except as permitted under Sections 107 or 108 of the 1976 United States Copyright Act, without either the prior written permission of the Publisher, or authorization through payment of the appropriate per-copy fee to the Copyright Clearance Center, 222 Rosewood Drive, Danvers, MA 01923, (978) 750-8400, fax (978) 750-4744. Requests to the Publisher for permission should be addressed to the Permissions Department, John Wiley & Sons, Inc., 605 Third Avenue, New York, NY 10158-0012, (212) 850-6011, fax (212) 850-6008, E-Mail: PERMREQ@WILEY.COM.

This publication is designed to provide accurate and authoritative information in regard to the subject matter covered. It is sold with the understanding that the publisher is not engaged in rendering professional services. If professional advice or other expert assistance is required, the services of a competent professional person should be sought.

Library of Congress Cataloging-in-Publication Data:

ISBN 0-471-36947-0

Printed in the United States of America.

10   9

Contents

Chapter 5   The Yield Test   97

Chapter 6   Standard Recipes   109

Chapter 7   Recipe Costing   117

Chapter 8   Characteristics of a Menu   131

Preface

The menu is the backbone of a foodservice operation. Developing a workable, quality menu is an important step in planning a profitable operation. The purpose of this book is to supply basic information to assist you in achieving this goal.

Fundamentals of Menu Planning provides a solid foundation in designing, costing, marketing, and merchandising a menu. It serves as a valuable resource for students, instructors, chefs, restaurateurs, and other foodservice professionals who wish to develop or redesign their menu.

Numerous tables and work forms are included to assist the menu planner. A collection of sample menus from some of the finest restaurants throughout the United States is also provided to aid the reader in assessing menu quality.

Features in this new edition include:

- Key words in bold
- Additional readings and software recommendations at the end of chapters
- An increased number of practice problems
- Updated information on Recommended Dietary Allowances and the U.S. Daily Allowance
- A diversified collection of regional menus
- Guidelines to designing a hot-cooking line
- A more extensive appendix that now includes *A Practical Guide to the Nutritional Labeling Laws for the Restaurant Industry* and the current *Accuracy in Menus* guidelines from the National Restaurant Association.

Fundamentals of Menu Planning accommodates the needs of an extensive and diversified audience looking to the successful design and implementation of an attractive and profitable menu.

Fundamentals of
Menu Planning

Chapter 1

Institutional, Industrial, and Commercial Menus

*T*o plan a profitable menu in the foodservice industry, the menu planner must be knowledgeable about foods, management, and financing. This chapter discusses facts and practical work experience that are essential in planning a profitable menu in the institutional, industrial, and commercial segments of the foodservice industry.

 *Objectives*

1. To give the student an understanding of the knowledge that a menu planner must have in order to prepare menus in each of the three foodservice segments

2. To help the student effectively apply the knowledge of planning menus to writing menus

3. To identify special characteristics in each of the foodservice segments

Background of a Menu Planner

Who can plan a menu? Anyone can plan a menu in its simplest form. The definition of a **menu** is simply "a listing of foods." If people are hungry, they can mentally plan a menu by choosing the foods they would like to eat. To plan a simple menu does not take years of experience and education. On the other hand, planning a successful and profitable menu for a commercial foodservice operation does take foodservice experience and a culinary education.

Menus planned for a commercial foodservice operation are different from those planned for an institutional or industrial foodservice operation. The person planning menus for an institutional, industrial, or commercial foodservice operation must be knowledgeable about a number of aspects of the foodservice industry. A **professional menu planner** must be knowledgeable about food, finances, and management. The menu planner must have a good understanding of all three of these areas in order to be able to plan a profitable menu. For a person to acquire enough knowledge in these three areas requires a combination of educational theory (know-how) and practical working experience (how-to) in each area.

When planning a menu, it is helpful and important for the menu planner to categorize the information into two categories: (1) necessary information and (2) helpful information. Information that is not necessary in menu planning for a commercial foodservice operation might be very necessary in menu planning for an institutional foodservice operation. For example, it is not essential to know the sodium dietary needs of customers when planning a menu for a commercial foodservice operation. Yet, this information would be necessary when planning a menu for a patient in an institutional foodservice operation.

In addition to knowing the type of **market** (customer) that will be patronizing the foodservice operation, the menu planner needs to have a knowledge of food, finances, and management when planning a menu.

Food

In the area of food, the menu planner must know the following:

1. The customer's likes and dislikes regarding food. Knowing which foods are preferred definitely helps the saleability of a product.
2. How to identify the various food products that are available in the markets.
3. How to explain the different criteria that establish the quality grades of food products.
4. The availability of the food products. Knowing when a food product is available helps keep food costs down and profits up.
5. How the food items are prepared, produced, plated, served, and consumed by the guest. This information allows the menu planner to specify the type of equipment necessary to produce the food product. This knowledge also will indicate the level of skill necessary for the cooks.
6. How the food product is packaged, shipped, received, and stored, as well as the shelf life of the product. This information helps

the menu planner to establish a quality menu for the foodservice operation.

7. Which foods are complementary to one another for the proper garnishing of dishes and for achieving an aesthetic and nutritionally balanced menu.

8. The yields of food products, which will help in setting up recipes.

9. How to do recipe conversions, how to merchandise, and how to market the food product.

10. How to cross-utilize products. Cross-utilization refers to using a menu product in more than one menu or in more than one product. For example, if a chef placed baked scallops with buttered bread crumbs on the menu, scallops should also appear in at least one or two more entrées, such as fried scallops or scallops in a casserole with cheese sauce. Just having scallops listed once on the menu would present product and cost problems, unless scallops were extremely popular and the amount purchased was used for only one entrée selection. Cross-utilization should be followed throughout the menu, not just in entrées. Most institutional menus use cross-utilization of food products exceptionally well.

Finances

The menu planner must understand the relationship between food costs and other expenses, such as labor and overhead.* The menu planner must be able to produce a menu that is profitable. Thus, the menu planner must understand how the portion cost affects the selling price. The prices on the menu must be appealing to the consumer, yet still allow the foodservice operation to make a profit.

The menu planner must know how to cost a recipe. Portion cost and markup must be related to volume in order to make a profit. **Recipe costing** is essentially finding a portion cost and marking it up to a selling price that the market will accept. A menu planner must have an awareness of how a sales history is developed and an understanding of

---

*Overhead refers to all costs that are not included in payroll costs or in food and beverage costs. Overhead costs include fixed expenses and variable expenses. Insurance is an example of a fixed overhead expense, because it does not fluctuate according to sales. No matter how much business a foodservice operation does, insurance costs stay the same. Equipment needs can vary with the amount of business done and would therefore be a variable overhead expense.

how to prepare a **sales mix** or a **scatter sheet,** which is used in fore-casting.* Knowing how to establish a **check average** and how to project annual sales are also essential. The menu planner must understand financing as it applies to the foodservice industry as a whole and to the menu in particular.

Management

To successfully design a profitable menu, it is important that the menu planner be aware of the foodservice owner's wants and needs. Profit, check average, type of operation, style of the menu, theme of the operation, style of service to be used, atmosphere, the mood that is to be achieved, the skill level of personnel, and the market all must be considered. The menu planner must know as much as possible about customers' food preferences and the price that customers are willing to pay in order to design the type of menu appropriate for a particular foodservice operation.

Institutional Foodservice

The institutional foodservice category is composed of

- Grade schools
- High schools
- Colleges and universities
- Private and federally funded hospitals
- Nursing homes and assisted-living facilities
- Correctional facilities
- Armed services

Each of these operations has its own dietary requirements that must be followed on the menu. The most important factor in planning an institutional menu is that the offerings must be nutritious. All institutional menus should include the five basic food groups: bread, cereal, rice and

---

*A scatter sheet is a record of the menu items that have been sold. Check average is the average amount of money that a person or a group of people will spend for a meal. Sales mix is a record of which menu items have been sold during a particular period of time.

pasta; vegetables; fruit; milk, yogurt, and cheese; meat, poultry, fish, dry beans, eggs, and nuts.

When planning a menu for any institution, the following factors should be considered:

1. The type of operation and the diet required by its patrons
2. Budget restrictions
3. Ages of the patrons
4. Food preferences of the patrons
5. Type of service needed
6. Hours of feeding
7. Storage area
8. Equipment needed to produce the menu
9. Government regulations
10. Religious and ethnic backgrounds of the patrons

Types of Operations and Required Diets

The menu offered will depend on the type of institutional operation. In a hospital setting the menu planner must follow strict dietary regulations that have been set by the registered dietician. The five main diets used in hospitals include

1. The Regular or house diet
2. The liquid diet
3. The mechanical soft diet
4. The diabetic diet
5. The cardiac diet

It is vital that a patient's meal be planned very carefully to assist the patient in making a faster recovery. If these diets are not followed as prescribed, illness or accidental death could result. (See Chapter 3 for a description of these diets)

Budget Restrictions

Most institutional foodservices today are operated by large foodservice companies, such as ARAMARK, ARA, Service Master, and Sodexho. The hospital, nursing home, or school will establish a *per diem* (dollar per day sum) under which the facility must operate. The menu need not stay within this sum each day; rather, it must remain within this budget over an accounting period, thus allowing the menu planner some flexibility in meal planning.

In most cases institutional cafeterias are set up on a break-even basis or on a 1 to 2 percent profit. The institution itself is not in business for the purpose of making a large profit in the foodservice operation. Thus, many institutional facilities charge very little for their food items.

Ages of Patrons

When a menu planner decides to plan a particular menu, the ages of the patrons who will consume the food must be considered. As we grow older our bodies require and are able to handle different foods. At infancy our digestive systems are very delicate and are able to digest only delicate foods. As our digestive systems mature, we are able to digest a much larger variety of foods. When we age, our digestive systems grow frail and we can digest a lesser variety of foods. Age has a direct effect on the items selected for a particular menu. Since hospital patients vary in age, the menu planner must have food items on the menu that appeal to all age groups, as well as making sure that these items together comprise a nutritionally balanced menu.

In an elementary or secondary school setting, the menu planner does not have to consider as many age groups as in a hospital. Planning menus for elementary and secondary school students is a much simpler task than planning menus for hospitals.

The college or university population presents more of a challenge to the menu planner. The ages of this group may vary from young adults to much older adults. College students also tend to be more demanding than young school children. Many students today are paying high tuition and room and board costs, and they expect to get adequate menu selections and quality food.

Food Preferences

Although, in many cases, institutions such as hospitals and schools are under strict dietary regulations or government regulations, the menu planner must take a careful look at what the patient or patron wants to eat within the institution. This process can be accomplished by a number of different methods.

A survey might be taken to determine which foods are popular or to determine which foods patrons hope to see on the menu in the future. The menu planner can review the surveys and make important evaluations that can help improve future menus. If possible, the menu planner should eliminate those foods that prove to be unpopular.

Another method of determining food preferences is to put suggestion boxes in the cafeteria. This idea does not work as well as the food survey. People will usually take a survey more seriously than placing suggestions in a box. At times an employer will make it mandatory for employees to fill out the survey, whereas suggestions in a suggestion box are entirely optional.

Type of Service Needed

In most institutional settings, the service is cafeteria style, which utilizes a tray line. Another popular service system is the **scatter system.** This system allows a large volume of people to move quickly, bypassing food stations from which they do not wish to select food. This system allows for much more customer involvement.

It is important to serve food that has good holding qualities, both hot and cold. In many institutions, hot food is served in steam tables and is allowed to continue to cook or to evaporate excess moisture. Stews, casseroles, and quiches are good examples of foods that have good holding qualities and that do not become overcooked or dried out if the temperature is properly set at a steam table. Items such as fried fish or roast beef can be served on a steam table, but only a few orders can be cooked or sliced at a time. Fried fish becomes soggy on the line if a cover is put over it. Roast beef tends to dry out and shrink when a cover is left on for a long period of time.

Cold items placed on a cafeteria service line should be placed on a bed of ice. Salads and dairy desserts require refrigeration units. It would be unwise to serve oysters or clams on the half shell because of their poor holding qualities; they lose their freshness when they are served at room temperature.

In a hospital, food is cooked and plated in the kitchen, placed in a refrigerated or heated cart, and transported to the patients' rooms. Another method of serving hot foods is to precook the food in the kitchen and to finish cooking it in a prep kitchen on the individual floor. In a hospital, it is very important to be accurate about serving foods at their proper temperatures in order to avoid the development of foodborne diseases, such as salmonella.

Note: Overall, when planning menus for institutional foodservice operations, the menu planner must look at the type of service to be used in order to maintain a quality food product.

Hours of Feeding

Within the institutional framework, hours of feeding will help determine the types of items that will be offered on the menu. If the hours of feeding are from 8 A.M. to 4 P.M., the menu planner must plan menus for breakfast and lunch. If an institution is operating a 24-hour feeding system, then breakfast, lunch, and dinner menus have to be planned.

Storage Area

In an institutional setting, the storage area that is available helps to determine the type of food that will be offered on the menu. In many cases, institutions have limited walk-in freezer space. Limited freezer space indicates that many items on the menu must either be fresh foods that require refrigerated space or canned foods that require storeroom facilities. The menu planner must take into consideration the amount and type of storage area available and balance the variety of food products on the menu accordingly.

Equipment Needs

Many institutions purchase their equipment first and then set up the menu. It is only afterward that management may realize that some of the equipment that it has procured is not necessary for the production of the menu. Always plan the menu first; then analyze it to decide the type of equipment needed to produce the menu. This part of the planning process is called a **foodservice equipment analysis.**

Most institutions have limited equipment because of budget restrictions. This fact makes menu planning even more important in the institutional setting.

Government Stipulations

In most institutional facilities, the government plays an important role in menu planning. In elementary and secondary schools, the foodservice systems must follow the school lunch requirements set up by the U.S. Department of Agriculture (USDA).

All branches of the armed services and veterans hospitals fall under strict government stipulations as well. It is important to keep abreast of the laws enacted by our governments (state and federal) that set dietary guidelines. Government financial aid may be suspended if laws or regulations are not followed when planning menus for government-funded institutions.

Religious and Ethnic Backgrounds

In institutional foodservice operations, religious and ethnic backgrounds of the people being served play an important role in the planning of menus. For example, in a Jewish hospital, strict cultural dietary requirements must be followed: dairy and meat products cannot be mixed and have to be kept in separate reach-ins; yet, eggs, fish, and vegetables, which are considered pareve, can be used with dairy or meat meals; lard or any other animal fat cannot be used, but soybean, palm, or vegetable oils are acceptable.

All nationalities have their own favorite foods. The Italian culture offers a variety of sausages, pasta products, and pastry products. The Irish culture offers a variety of stews, sauces and dessert coffees. It is important to offer employees or patients their preferred food items on the menu.

Industrial Foodservice

The industrial segment of the foodservice industry is composed of

- Corporations
- Companies
- Factories

and any other type of business that employs enough people to warrant the need for an in-plant foodservice operation.

For the menu planner to plan a successful menu within the industrial segment of the foodservice industry, the following factors must be taken into consideration:

1. Management's reasons for having a foodservice operation in-house
2. The food preferences of the employees to be fed
3. The type of work the employees are doing
4. The time allotted for meals
5. The amount of money the employees have to spend on meals

Profit

Management will spend money to make money. How does an industrial foodservice operation make a profit for management? It does so by keeping employees at or near their working stations during their meal period. Most employees are given a half-hour or an hour for their meal period. Employees will slow down or quit production five to ten minutes before eating, and many workers are five to ten minutes late in returning from eating when a business does not have a cafeteria or a foodservice operation in-house. Keeping the employees on the grounds of the business for meals helps to reduce the number of workers who return late from lunch, which increases production and, in turn, increases profits.

Operating Methods

The two methods of operating an industrial foodservice operation are for management to contract with a professional foodservice company to manage the operation or to take full responsibility of controlling the feeding system as a part of the business.

Contracting an outside professional foodservice company to handle the responsibility of feeding employees is popular and, in most cases, a profitable choice. There are several methods of feeding employees for which management may contract:

1. Computerized vending units
2. Full table service
3. Cafeteria service
4. Coffee-deli shops
5. Fast-food service

The two most important factors in choosing industrial foodservice establishments are offering fast service and providing menus that fit the needs of the employees.

Pricing

When pricing an industrial foodservice menu, management has a choice of setting the price in one of three ways:

1. Setting a large profit percentage (10 to 15 percent)
2. Setting a small profit percentage (1 to 2 percent)
3. Setting a break-even price (food is sold at a price that covers only the cost of the food, labor, and overhead, and the company does not make a profit)

Food Preferences

The menu planner must be familiar with employee food preferences in order to be able to plan a successful menu. A food survey should be conducted to determine employees' preferences in foods. Some employees may prefer a nutritional menu that includes poultry, fish, salads, fruits, and vegetables rather than a menu that includes hamburgers, hot dogs, sandwiches, and French fries. The survey should be conducted every three months in order to accommodate employee turnover and also because attitudes and tastes can change over time.

Type of Work

The menu planner needs to know the type of work that employees do. Are employees involved in physical activity, or are they sitting at their desks all day? This information helps to determine food portions, the amount and variety of foods to offer, and whether the items should be hearty and of a heavy calorie count. With jobs that require physical labor, employees are burning large amounts of calories, so the menu should offer a selection of foods that will replace lost calories. When employees do limited physical work, the menu selections should be light in calories and smaller in portion size.

Time

Knowing the amount of time allotted for the meal period is an important consideration. Food items that take a long time to prepare should not be included on the menu. Most employees are given only a half-hour or an hour to eat. If an item takes too long to produce, employees will not have enough time to finish their meals and will feel rushed. Thus, employees will be dissatisfied with the foodservice operation.

Price

The amount of disposable income that an employee has or is willing to spend for a meal on a daily basis may be limited. **Disposable income** is income that is available for the employee's use after federal, state, and city taxes, and personal bills have been paid. The menu planner should not select foods that have a high food cost and offer them at an even higher cost, because the average employee cannot afford to buy that product on a daily basis. The average employee does not want to spend more than $5 on each meal. The menu planner needs to offer food items that are of good quality and that are reasonably priced.

Commercial Foodservice

The commercial segment of the foodservice industry includes

- Hotels
- Restaurants
- Clubs
- Diners
- Fast-food operations
- Specialty shops
- Cafeterias
- Catering businesses
- Vending businesses
- Dinner theaters
- Delicatessens

In each of these foodservice operations, the menu planner must know management's point of view on the following:

1. How the operation is run
2. The type of clientele that management would like to attract (also known as the market)
3. Check average
4. Decor
5. Profit margin
6. Competition
7. Market trends

How the Operation Is to Run

Although there are many philosophies on how to operate a foodservice operation, there are three basic approaches: fast food, family, and fine dining. Management must recognize and have a full understanding of an operation's philosophy in order to achieve a maximum profit. Management must be completely dedicated to the philosophy selected and should avoid mixing different philosophies that would only serve to confuse the market.

Fast-Food Operation. Characteristics of the fast-food philosophy and operation are as follows:

- Low check average: $4 to $8
- High turnover of capacity and high volume of sales: the National Restaurant Association indicates a $1,000 to $5,000 sales amount per hour as high volume
- Limited square footage per person for dining: 7 to 9 square feet
- Bright lights: almost a shadowless lighting scheme
- The use of bold, bright, and loud primary colors: red, blue, and yellow
- Rapid employee movement, which tends to affect the customer's pace
- Limited seat comfort: the use of plastic nonmoveable seats provides less comfort than a cushioned, unfixed seat
- High noise (decibel) level: the use of nonacoustic materials (made from a hard substance, such as stone, brick, ceramic tile, or stainless steel)
- The use of styrofoam cups and plates, and paper napkins
- Limited menu: the selection of food items on the menu is limited to no more than 30 items, to reduce the time it takes for customers to read the menu and to decide on their orders

With this philosophy, the goal is to create an atmosphere that will allow the customer to eat and leave the foodservice operation as quickly as possible, usually within a 30-minute time period. Management must design the entire building (interior and exterior), in order to allow for rapid movement (flow) of customers. Every detail is geared toward getting the customer in and out of the foodservice operation as quickly as possible, without making the dining experience an uncomfortable, rushed, or negative one for the customer.

Family Operation. The objective of the family philosophy is designed to appeal to the market that falls between the fast-food and the fine-dining market. The term "family" indicates that management must take into consideration the desires of a wide range of customers—from grandchildren to grandparents. Characteristics of the family philosophy are as follows:

- Moderate check average: $8 to $15 per person
- Moderate turnover rate: one-and-a-half to two-and-a-half times per hour with a 100-seat capacity

- Square footage per person: 12 to 14 square feet
- Illumination (lighting) level: balanced, not dim or bright, but adequate
- Color scheme that incorporates a blend of pastel and bright colors
- Employee movement: prompt, not slow or too rapid
- Seating that is moderately comfortable; good quality chairs used
- Noise (decibel) level: ranges from 60 decibels (calm conversation) to 90 decibels (a loud argument), with a balanced use of acoustic and nonacoustic material
- Menu selections include 45 to 150 items: of all the types of menus, this type of menu takes the longest time to read, because graphics (such as photographs) accompany the description of the food products

This philosophy incorporates objectives from both the fast-food and fine-dining philosophies. The objective of not rushing customers is borrowed from the fine-dining philosophy, while the goal of not allowing the customer to take two hours to dine stems from the fast-food philosophy.

Fine Dining. The fine-dining philosophy is, in many ways, the opposite of the fast-food philosophy. The objective of the fine-dining philosophy is to provide the customer with a relaxing and pleasant dining experience. Characteristics of this philosophy include

- High check average: $45 to $100 per person
- A low turnover rate: a 100-seat capacity foodservice operation will have a three-quarter to one-and-a-half turnover capacity
- Square footage per person: 24 to 30 square feet to provide greater room and privacy, which allows the customer to be more relaxed
- Illumination level (lighting): low
- Colors selected are relaxing: pastel and earth-tone colors, such as tan and beige
- Employee movement in the dining room is not so rapid as to give a rushed impression and not so slow as to suggest indifference
- Seating is very comfortable: the use of fabric-padded seats provides more comfort
- Noise (decibel) level: a quiet, relaxing level of 30 to 70 decibels, facilitated by the use of soft acoustic material (wood, plants, carpets, fabric wallpaper, or other materials that absorb sound waves)

- Menu selections that are extensive (60 to 125 items) or limited (20 to 45 items), with more of a description accompanying the food items so as to enhance a person's appetite (when done correctly)
- High-quality interior decor: an atmosphere that encourages customers to relax, enjoy themselves, and spend money

It is important that a foodservice operation select only one philosophy. A combination of two or three philosophies during various hours of operation will only serve to confuse the customers and to deter them from identifying who you are and what you are all about. Very few foodservice operations can successfully combine philosophies and achieve a profitable margin.

Clientele

It is critical that the menu planner know the type of clientele for whom the menu is being planned. In the commercial segment, the primary motive for going into business is profit. To generate a maximum profit, the menu must satisfy the clientele.

The menu is one of management's ways of meeting the demands of the clientele. The menu needs to reflect these demands through food selections, price, and creativity.

Check Average

The *check average* is used to indicate the amount of money that people are spending. Foodservice managers use this information to evaluate and to set financial goals. If a foodservice operation sets a $12.50 check average per person as a goal prior to opening and is achieving only a $9.50 check average per person after it has opened, this information allows management to analyze why the check average is $3 short and to make the necessary changes. If management does not use this information, it will fall short of its financial goals, which could lead to indebtedness or failure.

Decor

The decor, or decoration, of a foodservice establishment should project an image with which the market can identify. All of the exterior and interior design (such as landscaping, painting of the building, color of the menu, the type of artwork, the wallpaper, the style of windows, the size and shape of the parking lot) must be done to accommodate the taste and style of the market. The first impression of the interior is derived from the appearance of the exterior of a property. A littered parking lot reflects a negative image—one of messiness and filth that is certainly not appealing or attractive to the customer who has never been to the establishment. To know what the market is looking for, you must do a market survey (see Chapter 2).

Profit Margin

Profit margin is the amount of money made on a food or beverage product. All food and beverage products generally have different profit margins, even if they have the same food cost percentage.

The profit margin is calculated when the food and beverage product is marked up from a preliminary selling price to a final selling price. For example, a slice of apple pie may cost $.35 to make. To make a profit, the slice of pie is sold for $1.75. The difference between $.35 and $1.75 is $1.40, which will pay for the ingredients, the cost of labor, the cost of the equipment, and the energy to make the pie, and will also contain a percentage for profit. When the price of the pie is increased to $2.25, the true margin of profit increases. If the price is lowered to $1.50, the margin of profit is lowered.

Management will always make a profit on the piece of apple pie if it is priced correctly. The question is, how much profit? The answer is determined by how much the market is willing to pay for the slice of pie. If the market will pay $3.50 for the slice of apple pie, then management can price it at $3.50 on the menu. (This topic is discussed further in Chapter 7.)

Competition

Competition in the foodservice industry, as in all business endeavors, keeps operations at a competitive edge. Management must keep its standards high or the customer will go elsewhere. Competition does the following:

1. It keeps the prices of menu items under control and competitive. A food operation will not overprice a product such as coffee, which is common among all operations.
2. It decreases advertising costs. If an independent foodservice operation locates next to a national foodservice chain organization, the independent operation can reduce spending on advertising, since the chain operation brings customers into and next to the independent foodservice operation.

Market Trends

The market is always changing. To be successful, the menu in a commercial foodservice operation needs to keep pace with the changes in the market. The menu planner and management must accurately forecast the demands of the market. This task is not simple. The following items must be considered: (1) new developments in food products, menu styles, decor concepts, as well as a variety of other trends occurring in the foodservice industry; (2) the economy and how it is affecting the market; and (3) the social needs of the market.

 Review Questions

1. What is the most important factor in planning a menu for an institution?

2. List three major areas with which a menu planner must be familiar in order to plan any type of menu.

3. Explain how foodservice managers will use the check average to determine financial goals?

4. List five elements that a menu planner must take into consideration when planning a menu for a commercial foodservice operation.

5. To accurately forecast changes within the market, which three areas must the menu planner and management recognize?

 Additional Readings

"A Road Map for 2000," *Restaurant Institution*, 1 January 2000, 66–74.

Wallace L. Rande, *Introduction to Professional Foodservice* (New York: John Wiley & Sons, 1996).

Chapter 2

Market Survey

*O*nce an owner has established a foodservice operational concept, a market survey needs to be done. The **market survey** is a detailed study of the people, the community, and the physical location of the foodservice establishment. This chapter discusses the elements that must be analyzed in a market survey.

Objectives

1. To determine what a market survey is
2. To identify how a restaurant owner should use a market survey
3. To illustrate the steps one needs to take in order to complete a market survey

Preliminary Steps

There are two basic steps in preparing a market survey. The first step is to establish the style and the type of foodservice operation or concept, and the second is to determine the community's need for such a business establishment. This planning should be done before any money is invested.

The foodservice planner needs to address many issues, such as

- Style of menu
- Type of clientele
- Type of cuisine

- Style of atmosphere
- Style of interior decor
- Expense of food, labor, and overhead
- Desired profit
- Amount of capital to be invested
- Regulations for operating on a daily basis
- Architect
- Lawyer
- Accountant
- Chef
- Staff

Information must be carefully collected and analyzed when one is preparing a market survey. The market survey indicates whether the community possesses the factors necessary to support an investor's foodservice operation.

The second step is to determine the community's needs or demands for such a foodservice operation. Most corporations, foodservice chains, and hotels complete step two, which is the key element in lowering the risk of failure.

Areas of Analysis

A market survey provides a detailed analysis of the following areas: the customer, the community, and the physical location of the foodservice operation.

The Customer

The customer is the most important element of a foodservice operation. The customer ultimately will make the operation a success or a failure. Key factors to know about the customer and how he or she affects foodservice operations include the following:

- Market or type of customer desired
- Age group
- Amount of disposable income

- Food preferences
- Social habits
- Educational level
- Religious orientation
- Ethnic background
- Predominant gender
- Occupational background
- Arrival pattern
- Preferred days for dining out

The Market. The **market,** or type of customer, that the foodservice operation wants to attract must first be considered. It is important to establish a particular market. Once a market has been established, every aspect of planning the foodservice operation will be geared toward that market. The more the foodservice planner knows about the customer, the greater the chance will be that the customer will experience a satisfying dining experience. Satisfied customers are the foodservice planner's key to a longer and more profitable existence.

Age Group. Knowing the age group of your market will help to determine the following:

- The type of cuisine and food selections to offer
- Prices
- Portion sizes
- Nutritional requirements
- Style of atmosphere
- Lighting level in the dining room
- Texture of the functional and decorative materials to be used
- Style of entertainment
- Accessibility of the operation and movement within it
- Type and intensity of background music
- Size of lettering on the menu

Amount of Disposable Income. **Disposable income** is the amount of income that is left after taxes and personal bills have been paid. Other names for disposable income are entertainment, fun, and luxury money. The greater the income your market has, the greater the amount of disposable income that will be available for dining at your establishment.

Food Preferences. Knowing the types of cuisine and the food selections within the cuisine that your market desires will save the operation money. It will allow management more free time to be creative with food items.

Social Habits. A knowledge of how your market likes to socialize aids in determining the type and style of entertainment needed.

Educational Level. People with a high level of education tend to be more receptive to trying something new. They also have a higher level of disposable income and dine out more often.

Religious Orientation. Some religious cultures have laws requiring how and what food items are to be consumed. Knowing customers' religious backgrounds can help to build up sales. One example is to offer a predominantly Catholic market a fish special on Fridays during Lent.

Ethnic Background. It is important to recognize the market's ethnic background in order to offer some favorite national dishes on the menu. It is not a realistic goal to open an Italian specialty restaurant in a heavily populated Chinese community. In all probability, the rate of success would not be very high.

Predominant Gender. A knowledge of whether your market is predominantly male or female will aid you in choosing the types of cuisine you plan to offer on the menu, the portion sizes, the balancing of calories and nutritional elements, and the decor. These factors aid you in determining the marketing and merchandising methods that are to be used to increase sales.

Occupational Background. The type of work that the customers in your market are engaged in throughout the day will help you to establish guidelines in the selection of foods to be placed on the menu and to determine the portion sizes. For example, if you are feeding people who do a lot of physical work, the food items and portion sizes should be heartier. Customers who are doing less physical work may prefer a food selection that has fewer calories and smaller portions. The amount of time individuals have for the luncheon period should influence the type of foodservice system used.

Arrival Patterns. Knowing the number of single people, couples, and parties of three or more and the time of day during which these various groups will be dining will aid your maître d' in setting up the dining room appropriately. Families with children tend to dine from 4:30 P.M. to 7 P.M., large groups without children tend to dine from 7 P.M. to 9 P.M., and couples tend to dine from 8 P.M. to 11 P.M. The proper arrangement of tables and chairs in the dining room that will accommodate each of these groups will result in a high turnover rate, thus increasing sales.

Preferred Days for Dining Out. Knowing which business days are popular and which ones are slower will help to establish the need for merchandising and marketing programs for the slow days. Fridays, Saturdays, and Sundays are very popular days for dining out, because people are often paid on Thursday or Friday and will have a greater amount of disposable income and time to go out. Mondays are usually the slowest days, because little, if any, disposable income is left over from the weekend, and there is very little time for dining out. These factors are only a sampling of the information that you should know about the market. The more that you know about the market, the easier it becomes for you to satisfy your customers' demands. Customers expect an enjoyable experience when they dine in a restaurant. Go one step farther and provide them with a *great* dining experience.

The Community

The geographic region, district, city, or town from which the majority of the foodservice operation's customers come is known as the **community.** Elements to study within the community include

- Growth rate
- Availability of liquor licenses
- Existence of competition
- Public services provided
- Requirements of the state Board of Health
- Number of families
- Potential for advertising

Growth Rate. If a community has a declining population, it is wise to discover the reason for the decline and to think twice about building or operating an establishment there. For example, it would be a mistake to build in a location where the unemployment rate is high. High unemployment means that businesses are closing and that people are moving elsewhere to find work. Other reasons not to choose a location include a high crime rate, high rents, and high taxes. An investor must take into consideration the amount of time it takes to collect data and to analyze the market survey, which is approximately six months to two years. It then takes another six to nine months to build the operation.

Availability of Liquor Licenses. Alcoholic beverages are one of the most profitable commodities that the foodservice industry has to sell. Obtaining a liquor license in some communities is a very expensive and difficult task. Each state and community has its own laws and procedures.

Foodservice investors usually start the process of obtaining a liquor license by completing the proper application. The investor is then placed on a waiting list. Once there is an opening for a license, the investor is called to go before a committee that regulates the license. The committee interviews the candidate and approves or denies the issuance of the license. Most communities, depending on state law, grant a limited number of licenses. The supply is low and the demand is high, thereby making the value and sometimes the cost of licenses high.

Another method of obtaining a liquor license is to buy a foodservice operation that already has a liquor license, which can be transferred to the new owner. The transferral of the license must be approved by the committee that regulates liquor licenses. All liquor licenses have to be renewed on an annual basis and may be revoked at any time if the investor breaks the law. It is important to check with local and state government agencies about liquor liability and costs.

Existence of Competition. There are two basic types of competition that the market survey must take into consideration: direct and indirect. **Direct competition** includes the foodservice operations that are directly related (similar) to your operation. They have a similar cuisine, decor, check average, capacity, and turnover rate. For example, if the investor wants to operate a steak house, the survey should indicate how many other steak houses there are in the community and which ones would be considered competition. **Indirect competition** consists of foodservice operations that are not similar to the investor's but are competing for the same customers. Competition analysis is done to determine if the community can support another operation.

Public Services Provided. To help calculate overhead expenses, the investor needs to know which public services are covered by tax dollars and which services will cost additional money. Police and fire protection are usually provided, but other types of services will vary from one community to another.

Requirements of the State Board of Health. The Board of Health serves to protect the public from circumstances that may place the public's health in danger. When the Board of Health inspects a foodservice operation, it is performing a public service for the community. If there is evidence of food contamination in a restaurant, the Board of Health may cite the operator or even shut down the operation.

Before any money is invested in the project, the Board of Health and the local fire department must look at the blueprints of the restaurant. Both departments can save time and money by indicating where there are violations in the project. Each community and state has different laws pertaining to health and fire codes. It is important to be aware of these laws.

Number of Families. The number of families in a community usually indicates whether the community has a stable and/or a growing population. When there are many families with children in a community, there is usually a large school system. The school system is a good source for an effective merchandising program. For example, if the investor's market is families, a favorite dessert contest might provide a great promotional program. The students in grades four, five, and six could draw posters of their favorite desserts and give the desserts names. The foodservice would choose the winner at the restaurant and would give prizes to all who participate.

Potential for Advertising. One of the key elements to a successful advertising program is communicating on the customers' level. If the investor is trying to attract business executives, the restaurant may place an ad in the *Wall Street Journal*. This ad would not be effective if the foodservice planner were trying to attract a different type of clientele. A second key element is to analyze the community's newspapers, radio stations, periodicals, and television stations. The amount of exposure or circulation that each advertising method gives is important. Enough money should be set aside in the budget to run an effective advertising campaign. Planning ahead for advertising can allow for promotions throughout the year.

The Location

One of the first steps in choosing a location is to determine future needs. Planning ahead is vital when choosing a location. The needs of a foodservice operator who wants to establish a chain of operations differ from those of a foodservice operator who wants to open a single operation. Knowing what you want and need before looking for a location helps to eliminate much wasted time and frustration. An excellent location alone will not make your foodservice operation a success, nor will a poor location necessarily guarantee failure. The entire operation must be first-rate. When selecting a location, you should analyze the population of the state, city, and suburban communities before arriving at a decision. Population trends may shift drastically in a city if the city is dependent on a particular industry for its financial survival. When a factory or a company goes out of business, the people in that city or community must travel elsewhere for work. The foodservice operation that depends on these people would also be closing its doors. It is important to note how fast or slow a state, city, or suburban community is growing. Refer to Figure 2-1 for other points in analyzing the location of a foodservice operation.

Other Things to Consider

Zoning. There are three types of zones: residential, industrial, and commercial. Each zone has zoning ordinances that must be obeyed. One cannot freely erect any type of building in a residential zone. This zoning restricts business developments for the safety of the residents who live in the zone. Industrial zones are established for large-volume companies, and commercial zones are established for small-volume companies. Check with the Zoning Board to find out what types of restrictions are placed on the land on which you plan to operate your business. You must comply with the Zoning Board regulations before opening your operation. As the population changes in a community, so will zoning laws.

Area Characteristics. The type of neighborhood in which your establishment is located will have a great effect on your business. If the neighborhood has a high crime rate, if pollution is evident, or if your neighborhood opposes development, you will find it difficult to succeed.

Physical Characteristics. Analyzing the land (soil) will give you an idea about the development that is needed and the cost. For landscaping purposes, have the topsoil of the property analyzed for nutrient and mineral content. Take note of the direction in which the land slopes, for proper drainage. Also note large rocks and trees that might have to be cleared, which add to the cost of the project.

Have a **percolation test** done on the land to see how long it takes for water to be absorbed into the soil for proper drainage. A percolation test is done by placing small holes throughout the lot below the frost line (6 to 10 feet), filling them with water, and timing how long it takes

(1) Zoning
    Current zoning of site
    Use permits needed
    Height restrictions
    Front line setback
    Side yard requirements
    Back yard requirements
    Restrictions on signs
    Parking requirements
    Other restrictions
(2) Area characteristics
    Type of neighborhood
    Type of businesses
    Growth pattern
    Proposed construction
    Other available sites
    Zoning of adjacent sites
(3) Competition
    Number of food facilities in drawing
        area of site
    Number of seats
    Type of menu offered
    Method of service
    Check averages
    Number of cocktail lounges
    Quality of drinks
    Bar service available at tables
    Annual sales
(4) Physical characteristics
    Type of topsoil
    Type of subsoil
    Depth of water table
    Presence of rocks
    Load-bearing capacity
    Direction of slopes
    Surface drainage
    Percolation test results
    Natural landscaping
    Other features
(5) Size and shape (including sketch)
    Length
    Width
    Total square feet
    Square footage needed for building
    Square footage needed for parking
    Space for other requirements
(6) Costs
    Cost per front foot
    Cost per square foot
    Total cost of site
    Cost of comparable sites nearby
    Costs for land improvements
    Real estate taxes
    Other taxes
(7) Utilities
    Location, cost, and size or capacity of
        Storm sewer

    Sanitary sewer
    Gas lines
    Water lines
    Electricity
    Steam
(8) Streets
    Basic patterns
    Width or lanes
    Paved
    Curbs and gutters
    Sidewalks
    Lighting
    Public transportation
    Grades
    Hazards

	Distance	Driving Time
(9) Positional characteristics		
Distance and driving time to		
Central business district		
Industrial centers		
Shopping centers		
Residential areas		
Recreational areas		
Sporting events		
Educational facilities		
Special attractions		
Other activity generators		

(10) Traffic information
    Distance to nearest intersection
    Traffic characteristics

Traffic counts	Day	Time	Count
Site street			
Adjacent streets			

(11) Visibility
    Anticipated changes
    Distances of sight from
        Left
        Right
        Across
    Obstructions
    Location of signs
(12) Services
    Quality of police protection
    Quality of fire protection
    Location of hydrant
    Availability of trash pickup
    Availability of garbage pickup
    Other services required
(13) General recommendations
    Suitability
    Desirability
    Other recommendations

FIGURE 2-1 Checklist for Analyzing the Location of a Foodservice Operation. (*From E. A. Kazarian*, Foodservice Facilities Planning, *3rd ed., New York: John Wiley & Sons, 1989.*)

the water to be absorbed into the soil. If it takes more than 20 minutes, usually the land will not pass its percolation test and the investor will not be allowed to obtain a building permit, because the land is deemed unsafe for building. The percolation test also will indicate the type of soil, rock, and clay that are under the topsoil.

Size, Shape, and Costs. The Department of Health and the Zoning Board must see renovation or new construction blueprints. The blueprints must be printed by a registered architect to be approved. Both of these organizations will want to make sure that the building material and total square footage meet their regulations. The architect also must see that all materials are purchased at lower prices and are of the best quality.

Streets and Traffic Information. Street patterns, such as one-way streets, should be noted. Foodservice operations located on one-way streets usually do not have as much traffic as operations located on two-way streets. Drivers usually have better access to an operation if it is on a two-way street. The width of the street and the width of the driveway are important as well. Make sure delivery trucks can enter and exit your establishment easily.

Intersections always slow down potential customers. When people are stopped at an intersection for the traffic light or a stop sign, they have time to look around and notice your business. The slower the speed limit is, the more opportunity people have to observe your operation. Traffic counts of how many cars pass the location of your establishment can be obtained through the city transportation office. The more cars pass by, the greater the potential will be for customers.

Sales Generators. Civic centers, theaters, and shopping malls can generate sales.

Visibilty. A foodservice operation with high visibility reduces the cost of advertising. A property that is located in a city and is hidden by a building requires more advertising in order to let people know where it is located.

Parking. Provide adequate parking to attract customers. The parking area must be designed to accommodate the following:

- Customers
- Employees

- Lights
- Dumpsters
- Delivery trucks
- Landscaping

Snow and Trash Removal. Removal of snow and trash is expensive. It is best to check local rates and methods of removal.

Obtaining Information for the Market Survey. The information for completing a market survey should be collected from the following sources:

- National Restaurant Association
- Chamber of Commerce
- Better Business Bureau
- Small Business Association (SBA)
- Public library
- Economic Development Department of your city or state
- City Hall
- Tourist Information Bureau
- U.S. Census Bureau
- Banking and financing corporations
- Real estate agencies
- Surveys you conduct
- Internet, state web sites of Economic Development Agencies

Review Questions

1. What is the purpose of a percolation test?

2. What is disposable income?

3. What is a market survey?

4. What are the two methods of obtaining a liquor license?

5. What are three elements to be analyzed about the community?

Additional Readings

John A. Drysdale, *Profitable Menu Planning* (Englewood Cliffs, NJ: Prentice-Hall, 1994).

Paul J. McVety, Sue Marshall, and Bradley J. Ware *The Menu and the Cycle of Cost Control* (Dubuque, IA: Kendall/Hunt Publishing Co., 1997).

The Sourcebook of Zip Code Demographics, 10th ed. (CACI Marketing Systems, 1995).

Tableservice Restaurant Trends. (Chicago, IL; The National Restaurant Association, 1998).

Chapter 3

Nutrition and Menu Planning

*T*his chapter examines the role of nutrients in foods and their relationship to health. The planning of therapeutic diets is discussed. Methods to improve the nutrient quality of foods that are offered in a foodservice institution are also examined.

Objectives

1. To provide students with an exposure to the basics of nutrition
2. To discuss the relationship of nutrition and health
3. To illustrate how menus can be nutritious and still profitable to the foodservice operation

Nutrition Basics

Nutrition is the study of how food is used by the body. Food is composed of nutrients, which are chemical compounds that are needed for survival. Some of these are essential nutrients, which cannot be made in the body and which must be supplied by food or supplements. Examples of essential nutrients are minerals, such as iron and calcium, vitamins, and certain amino acids that combine to form protein. Without a source of these essential nutrients, good health cannot be maintained. There are other nutrients that are equally important for survival, but these essential nutrients can be synthesized in the body, provided that the raw materials are available. Examples of this type of nutrient are the fatty substance, lecithin, and the nonessential amino acids.

The six major nutrient groups are:

1. Proteins
2. Carbohydrates
3. Fat
4. Vitamins
5. Minerals
6. Water

Proteins provide calories, synthesize new body tissue during growth, and replace worn-out cells. Proteins also form hormones, enzymes, and antibodies, which are required for performing numerous bodily processes and for maintaining immunity to diseases.

Carbohydrates, which include sugars, starches, and fiber, are most important as an energy source for the body, particularly the nervous system. Dietary fiber, which is mostly indigestible carbohydrates, helps to regulate the movement of food through the digestive tract.

Fats are a very concentrated energy source, providing more than twice as many calories as an equal amount of protein or carbohydrate. Some fats are *saturated*, which means that their chemical structure contains the maximum number of hydrogen atoms (i.e., they are saturated with hydrogen). These fats are solid and tend to be found in animal products. *Unsaturated fats* are missing some hydrogen atoms in their chemical structure and are liquid at room temperature. The missing hydrogens are replaced with chemical structures called double bonds. If a fat has one double bond, it is a *monounsaturated* fat; if it has two or more double bonds, it is a *polyunsaturated* fat. Commonly used monounsaturated fats include olive oil, and corn, soybean, and sunflower oils. Unsaturated fats can be turned into solid, saturated fat by a process called **hydrogenation.** Unsaturated fats that have been hydrogenated and are therefore made more saturated convey many of the same health risks as fats that are naturally saturated.

Vitamins are chemical compounds that are involved in various metabolic reactions in the body (see Table 3-1). They are divided into two groups:

1. Fat-soluble vitamins: vitamins A, D, E, and K
2. Water-soluble vitamins: B vitamins and vitamin C

Minerals are crystalline chemical elements that comprise about 4 percent of a person's weight. Like vitamins, they perform various functions (see Table 3-2). Calcium, phosphorous, sodium potassium, mag-

Table 3-1 **VITAMINS**

Vitamin (Chemical Name) Food Sources	Functions	Deficiency Symptoms
Vitamin A (retinol, carotene) liver, butter, carrots, pumpkin	Enables eyes to adjust to changes in light; maintains cells of skin, eyes, intestines, and lungs	Night blindness; keratinization (formation of thick, dry layer of cells on skin and eyes)
Vitamin D (ergocalciferol, cholecalciferol) fortified milk, fish livers	Enhances calcium and phosphorus absorption	Rickets in children; osteomalacia in adults
Vitamin E (alpha-tocopherol) vegetable oils	Acts as an antioxidant, protecting substances damaged by exposure to oxygen	Rare, but may cause hemolytic anemia in premature infants
Vitamin K (phylloquinone menaquinone) dark green leafy vegetables, liver	Essential for blood clotting	Rare, causes hemorrhaging
Vitamin B1 (thiamin) pork, whole grains	Part of coenzyme, thiamin pyrophosphate, which is needed for metabolism of carbohydrates and fat	Beriberi, which results in appetite loss, nausea, vomiting, impaired heart function
Vitamin B2 (riboflavin) milk, green vegetables, cheese	Part of coenzymes, flavin mononucleotide and flavin adenine dinucleotide, which aid in the release of energy from fat, protein, and carbohydrate	Ariboflavinosis, with symptoms of cracked and dry skin around nose and mouth
Vitamin B3 (niacin) milk, whole grains, nuts	Part of nicotinamide adenine dinucleotide and nicotinamide adenine dinucleotide phosphate, which are needed for energy release in cells	Pellagra, causing dermatitis, diarrhea, dementia
Vitamin B6 (pyridoxine) liver, bananas, wheat bran	Vital for amino acid synthesis and breakdown	Abnormal protein metabolism, poor growth, convulsions, anemia, decreased antibody formation
Vitamin B12 (cobalamin) almost all animal products none in plant products)	Aids in formation of nucleic acids; needed for proper red blood cells development	Pernicious anemia, which causes megaloblastic anemia and spinal cord degeneration
Folic acid dark green, leafy vegetables	Needed for cell growth and reproduction and amino acid metabolism	Megaloblastic anemia, which is characterized by abnormally large red blood cells that have failed to mature properly

Table 3-1 (CONTINUED)

Vitamin (Chemical Name) Food Sources	Functions	Deficiency Symptoms
Biotin egg yolk, liver, nuts	Part of enzyme system, acetyl coenzyme A, which is necessary for producing energy from glucose, and forming fatty acids, amino acids, nucleic acids, and glycogen	Very unlikely, but could cause dermatitis, fatigue, loss of appetite
Pantothenic acid liver, eggs, peas, peanuts	Part of coenzyme A, which is involved in releasing energy from carbohydrates, fat, and protein; also part of enzyme needed for fatty acid synthesis	Unlikely; causes fatigue, headaches, muscles cramps, poor coordination
Vitamin C (ascorbic acid) citrus fruits, broccoli, strawberries	Needed for formation of collagen, which binds cells together, maintains elasticity and strength of blood vessels	Scurvy, with symptoms of bleeding and swollen gums, poor wound healing

nesium, sulfur, and chlorine are considered macronutrients, because they are present in the body in relatively large amounts. The micronutrients, or trace minerals, are thus named because of the extremely minute quantities found in the body. These micronutrients include iron, zinc, selenium, manganese, copper, iodine, and fluorine, to name a few. Altogether, there are 22 minerals that are known to be required.

Water, often taken for granted, is perhaps the most vital nutrient. While a person can survive for weeks or months without the other essential nutrients, a complete deprivation of water would cause death within a few days. Water dissolves and transports nutrients into, throughout, and from the body. It also regulates body temperature, lubricates joints, is involved in chemical reactions, and helps cells retain their shape.

Meeting Nutrient Needs

In order to receive adequate supplies of all the essential nutrients, it is important to eat a variety of foods. The Five Basic Food Groups Plan was developed as a convenient method for ensuring that this goal is met. It divides foods into five groups, based on their nutrient content and recommends the number of servings from each group. The Five Basic Food Groups Plan is detailed in Figure 3-1. Note that there is no food group for fats and oils and for many sweets.

Table 3-2 MINERALS

Mineral/Food Source	Functions	Deficiency Symptoms
Calcium milk, soybeans	Forms bones and teeth; essential for blood clotting; involved with nerve stimulation, muscle contraction, and good muscle tone	Osteoporosis, causing bones to become brittle and break easily; most likely to occur in postmenopausal women
Phosphorus meat, poultry, carbonated drinks	Combines with calcium to form bones and teeth; part of nucleic acids; part of substances that store and release energy	Unlikely, but can cause weakness, appetite loss, bone pain
Sodium table salt, cured meats, processed foods	Dissolved in the water outside cells where it maintains osmotic balance and regulates water balance; aids in transmitting nerve impulses	Very unlikely; causes cardiac arrest, convulsions
Potassium oranges, bananas, winter squash	Dissolved in water inside cells to maintain osmotic balance and regulate water balance; aids in transmitting nerve impulses	Irregular heart beat
Magnesium milk, whole grains, nuts	Needed to conduct nerve impulses; catalyst in many energy transfer and release reactions	Nerve tremors, convulsions, behavioral disturbances
Sulfur Eggs, cabbage, meat	Component of several amino acids and vitamins	Extremely unlikely
Chlorine table salt, meat, milk, eggs	Part of hydrochloric acid in stomach, which aids in digestion and absorption; when bound to sodium or potassium, involved in maintaining water balance in cells	Loss of appetite, poor growth, weakness
Iron liver, nuts, meat, spinach	Part of hemoglobin that carries oxygen in the blood; part of myoglobin that transfers oxygen from hemoglobin to muscle cells	Anemia that causes low hemoglobin levels and fatigue
Zinc meat, fish, milk	Needed for collagen formation; component of insulin	Impaired growth, wound healing, sexual dysfunction and taste dysfunction
Selenium meat, seafood, wheat	Antioxidant	Not observed in humans
Manganese cereal, legumes	Needed for bone development	No deficiency observed in humans; in deficient animals, it causes slowed growth, deformities, and interferes with reproduction

Table 3-2 (CONTINUED)

Mineral/Food Source	Functions	Deficiency Symptoms
Copper nuts, dried beans, liver	Needed for hemoglobin and connective tissue formation	Anemia

Iodine
  saltwater fish and shellfish,
  iodized salt
	Part of thyroid hormones that regulate basal metabolism	Goiter

Fluorine
  fluoridated water, sardines,
  tea
	Strengthens bones and teeth	Teeth less resistant to decay

Following the suggested Five Basic Food Groups Plan recommendations in the strictest sense could provide a nutritious diet with as few as 1,000 calories. Many people have higher caloric needs that can be met by increasing the number of servings from the food groups and by adding foods that are not part of the food plan.

Recommended Dietary Allowance

More specific than the Five Basic Food Groups Plan is the *Recommended Dietary Allowance* (RDA), the suggested level of daily consumption for protein, 11 vitamins, and 7 minerals. The RDA was developed by the Food and Nutrition Board of the National Research Council—National Academy of Sciences and is intended to be a generous recommendation that should meet the nutrient needs of practically all healthy persons. The RDA is grouped by age and sex; recommendations also are given for pregnant and lactating females. Recommendations for calorie intake and a range of estimated safe and adequate levels for additional vitamins and minerals are also included in the RDA. The RDA is revised approximately every five years, at which time, changes in the suggested nutrient intake levels might be made, based on recent research findings.

Nutrition Labeling

The *U.S. Recommended Daily Allowance*, developed by the Food and Drug Administration, was based on the 1968 revision of the Recommended Dietary Allowance. This was the first labeling system for the listing of nutrient levels on food labels. In 1990, the Nutrition Labeling and Education Act, and regulations set by the Food and Drug Ad-

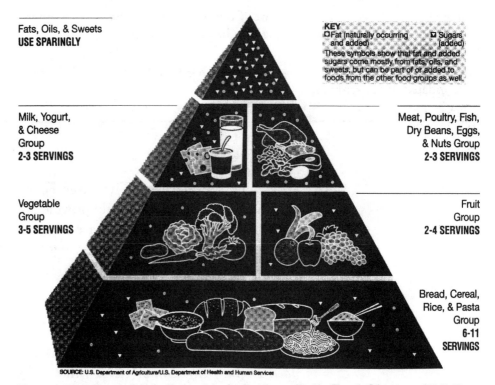

FIGURE 3-1 Food Guide Pyramid: A Guide to Daily Food Choices. *(U.S. Department of Agriculture, Human Nutrition Information Service, August 1992, Leaflet No. 572.)*

ministration and the U.S. Department of Agriculture established that, by the year 1994, all packaged foods would be required to carry labels listing a food's nutritional content (see Appendix F).

The Relationship of Nutrition to Health

Americans are becoming increasingly aware that nutrition has a strong impact on health. Not only will adequate amounts of nutrients promote good health by preventing deficiencies, but also good nutrition may also help in the prevention of chronic diseases and in increasing longevity.

Preventing Deficiencies

Fortunately in the United States, our abundant food supply makes it possible for most individuals to be well nourished. However, obtaining enough of certain nutrients may still be a problem for some groups of people. Females of reproductive age often receive too little iron in their diets, making iron-deficiency anemia the most common nutrient deficiency in this country. In addition, females are frequently victims of osteoporosis, which develops after menopause, usually after years of a chronically low calcium intake. Other vulnerable groups include the following:

- The elderly, whose physical and economic restrictions often limit their ability to eat a nutritious diet
- The poor, because they often cannot afford an adequate diet
- Chronic eaters, whose goal of thinness often precludes eating nutritiously

Avoiding Chronic Diseases

Many chronic diseases in this country are the result of a combination of overnutrition and the advances of technology that make life easier. Cardiovascular, or heart disease is one such example. Although deaths from heart disease have declined since the 1960s, it is still the number one killer in the United States. The underlying condition that causes heart disease is *atherosclerosis,* or hardening of the arteries. Atherosclerosis is characterized by the presence of fatty deposits, called *plaques,* in the arteries. As these plaques develop, they progressively increase blockage in the arteries, causing chest pain (*angina pectoris*), heart attacks, and strokes. Extensive research has identified high blood cholesterol levels, cigarette smoking, high blood pressure, obesity, and physical inactivity as some of the major contributors to the development of atherosclerosis.

Risk of heart disease is increased when blood cholesterol levels are above 200 milligrams per 100 milliliters of blood. It is important to know the amounts of "good" (HDL) and "bad" (LDL) cholesterol in the blood as well as total blood cholesterol. A high proportion of LDL cholesterol increases the risk of heart disease, whereas a high proportion of HDL lowers the risk of heart disease. To lower blood cholesterol levels, the National Cholesterol Education Program (NCEP) recommends a diet that provides less than 300 milligrams of cholesterol per day and that reduces fat intake to no more than 30 percent of energy, and saturated fat to less than 10 percent. Of this allowance, less than one-third should be saturated fat. Recent research has also suggested the possibility that various other dietary changes may lower the risk of cardiovascular disease. These include the highly unsaturated fatty acids (omega-3 fatty acids) found in salmon and other fatty fish, dietary fiber (particularly oat bran and pectin), and monounsaturated fats such as olive oil.

Some forms of cancer have been linked to diet as well. Research studies abound suggesting that a high-fiber diet can prevent cancer of the colon. The risk of lung cancer may be reduced by eating generous amounts of foods containing vitamin E and beta-carotene (the orange pigment in vegetables that is converted to vitamin A). A high-fat intake has been implicated as a risk factor for breast, colon, and prostate cancers. The National Cancer Institute has released dietary guidelines that are designed to reduce the incidence of cancer and cancer-related deaths. These recommendations include raising fiber to 20-30 grams per day, eating more fruits and vegetables, and lowering fat and alcohol consumption.

A medical problem that plagues approximately 25 percent of adult Americans is *high blood pressure,* or *hypertension.* Called the silent killer, because it usually has no symptoms, high blood pressure can cause strokes, heart attacks, and kidney failure. A high sodium intake is frequently linked with high blood pressure, and diet therapy often includes sodium restriction. Most people consume far more sodium than they need; one reason is the prevalence of sodium in our food supply. Some foods naturally contain a lot of sodium, but the vast majority of our foods comes from processed foods that contain salt and other sodium-containing ingredients added for flavor. The American Heart Association recommends a maximum daily intake of 3,000 milligrams of sodium, which easily can be exceeded by a person who uses processed foods or eats frequently in restaurants and other foodservice establishments.

Obesity is a problem that afflicts approximately one-fourth of adults in the United States. Not only does it cause numerous social problems, but also it contributes to a myriad of health problems. These health problems include heart disease, diabetes, high blood pressure, and even cancer. There are numerous causes for obesity, both physiological and environmental. A sedentary lifestyle, combined with a high calorie intake, most certainly contributes to the development of obesity in many individuals. Unfortunately, in this country, people are constantly bombarded with calorie-laden meals and snacks. This, combined with the conveniences of modern life, creates a vicious cycle that increases calorie intake and decreases calorie expenditure, resulting in obesity. A good treatment plan not only includes a lower-calorie, nutritionally balanced diet, but also changes an individual's eating behavior and encourages physical activity.

Nutritional Implications for Menu Planning

When planning the menu for an institutional, industrial, or commercial foodservice operation, it is beneficial to the clientele to take into consideration their nutrient needs. Even though some people are unconcerned about nutrition, an ever-growing number want the opportunity to select nutritious foods.

If a foodservice operation offers nutritious food, it helps to heighten the patrons' awareness of nutrition. A nutrient breakdown and general nutrition information about items found on the menu, which would be printed on the menu; circulating a health-oriented newsletter; and offering nutrition seminars are just a few ways to increase interest in healthful eating. The staff also should possess some knowledge about nutrition, so that they can answer questions about the foods they are serving.

Educating foodservice personnel about nutrition can be achieved by organizing seminars and encouraging employees to take courses on this subject.

Institutional Foodservice

In some cases, the foodservice operation must follow strict guidelines when planning the menu. For instance, the U.S. Department of Agriculture's National School Meals Program delineates a nutrient-based analysis system that must be followed weekly in all public elementary and secondary schools. The menus must provide, over the course of this period, no more than 30 percent of total calories as fat and no more than 10 percent of total calories as saturated fat. Lunch menus must provide one-third of the RDA for calories, protein, iron, calcium, vitamin A, and vitamin C. Breakfast menus must provide 25 percent of the same nutrients.

Careful attention must be paid to meal preparation. Meal patterns that provide many essential nutrients also can be high in fat, sodium, and sugar, depending on how the food is prepared. By offering broiled chicken, baked potatoes, a salad bar, fresh fruit, and low-fat milk instead of fried chicken nuggets, French fries, canned vegetables, cake, and whole milk, a school lunch program can provide students with a healthy midday meal. While both these meals are similar in calorie content, the former provides much lower amounts of fat and sodium, as well as higher levels of protein, fiber, vitamins, and minerals.

While the government has not set guidelines for college foodservice organizations, it is the responsibility of these organizations to provide nutritious meals for students, especially since the cafeteria is the sole provider of food for many of them. The Five Basic Food Groups Plan is a good foundation for planning a college menu, as well as for providing a wide variety of foods that are low in fat, cholesterol, sodium and sugar. Some college and university foodservice organizations set a good example by offering vegetarian or ethnic fare to their students.

Hospitals are not subject to governmental regulations when they are planning patients' menus. However, they are influenced by the patients' dietary restrictions, which may vary from mild to severe. Some types of diets served in a hospital include the following.

Regular or House Diet. A patient on a regular or house diet faces no restrictions and can freely choose from items on the menu. Offering a variety from the five food groups helps to ensure that the patient will receive adequate amounts of nutrients.

Liquid. A clear liquid diet is usually the first nourishment that a postoperative patient receives. It is also used in preparation for bowel surgery or examinations, as well as when there is an acute disturbance in gastrointestinal function. It is not nutritionally balanced; thus, it should not be used for an extended period of time, unless supplements are added. The foods allowed on this diet include broth, bouillon, gelatin, strained fruit juices, coffee, tea, carbonated beverages, and sugar. A full liquid diet is much more nutritionally balanced, because it includes a much wider variety of foods. All items on a clear liquid diet are allowed, as well as all other beverages, strained cream soups, eggs, certain hot cereals, ice cream, sherbert, custards, puddings, margarine, butter, and all spices. This diet is prescribed if there is difficulty with chewing or swallowing, and it is also used postoperatively.

Mechanical, Soft Diet. A mechanical, soft diet that is low in sodium is indicated for congestive heart failure, liver and kidney failure, and in the management of high blood pressure. The degree of restriction may vary from a "no-added-salt" diet (about 4,000 milligrams), which eliminates very salty foods and the salt shaker, to a 250-milligram sodium diet, which is extremely restrictive and requires the use of special low-sodium foods.

Diabetic Diet. A diabetic diet is necessary when an individual does not produce enough insulin and blood sugar levels become dangerously high. This diet restricts the use of sugars, fat, and cholesterol, and encourages a high-complex carbohydrate intake. The diet plan usually consists of three meals and two snacks each day. To allow variety in the diet, permitted foods are divided into the following exchange groups: starch/bread, meat and meat substitutes, vegetables, fruit, milk, and fat. If, for example, a diabetic is allowed a starch/bread exchange at a meal, he or she may choose one slice of bread, one-half cup of rice, or a small potato. Because this diet is well balanced and provides a good deal of variety, some hospitals use it for planning weight loss regimens as well.

Cardiac Diet. The purpose of the cardiac diet is to lower the levels of cholesterol and fat in the blood. In general, cholesterol and total fat are reduced. The proportion of unsaturated fat is raised. In some cases, sodium, sugar, and alcohol might be restricted. Foods to be avoided in this diet usually include egg yolks, fatty meats, most cheeses, whole milk products, fried foods, and high-fat sweets, such as cakes and cookies.

Industrial Foodservice

Because having a foodservice operation available on-site for employees is often more convenient and inexpensive for employees, an industrial foodservice organization is usually serving a "captive" audience. The nature of the work that employees perform plays a role in determining the menu. For example, if many of the employees have desk jobs that require little physical exertion, foods that are lower in calorie and are less filling, such as salads and soups, may be preferred. If, on the other hand, employees are engaging in heavy physical labor, high-calorie foods will be required to provide them with the necessary energy. In this case, offering meals such as stews and substantial sandwiches would be in the best interest of the employees. A variety of foods that are low in fat and high in complex carbohydrates should be adequate to meet the needs of both sedentary and physically active employees.

Commercial Foodservice

It is profitable for a commercial foodservice operation to offer nutritious menu items, because many patrons now are demanding dishes that are lower in calories, fat, cholesterol, and sodium. A commitment to healthful food is demonstrated by the concept of "spa cuisine," which was developed by New York City's Four Seasons restaurant and the Columbia-Presbyterian Medical Center. Spa cuisine selections are made with less oil, salt, and sugar, and offer the customer a delicious meal that is both lower in calories and more healthful. Other restaurants, from the expensive and the exclusive to the fast-food operations, have followed suit, and now it is no longer unusual to find a selection of nutritionally balanced dishes on a restaurant's menu.

Even when a restaurant does not offer its own version of spa cuisine, it is still possible for that establishment to cater to a customer's special needs or preferences. Serving sauces or dressings on the side; decreasing the amount of butter and salt added to vegetables and broiled items; and offering fresh fruit as an alternative to rich desserts are just a few of the many ways in which a restaurant can accommodate its patrons without having to revamp its cooking methods or menu.

Ingredients and Preparation

The ingredients and preparation methods that a foodservice operation uses will have a vast effect on the food's nutrient content. It is desirable to maximize the amount of vitamins, minerals, and fiber and to minimize calories, fat, cholesterol, sodium, and sugar.

Vitamins are very fragile substances that can be destroyed by exposure to acid, alkali, heat, light, and air. The enzymes that are naturally present in foods can cause destruction, and the water-soluble vitamins can leach into the cooking water and be lost when the water is discarded. Frozen fruits and vegetables are generally higher in vitamins than their fresh or canned counterparts, due to the fact that they are usually frozen immediately after harvesting and have undergone minimal processing. Fresh foods, on the other hand, may travel great distances to market, and it can be days or even weeks before they are sold "fresh." During this lag time, a large percentage of vitamins may be lost. Canned foods experience harsher processing conditions and might not be eaten for months or years after harvesting.

Tailoring a foodservice operation's cooking methods to minimize vitamin loss can be achieved by adhering to the following guidelines:

1. Avoid overcooking food.
2. Steam, stir-fry, or microwave foods instead of boiling them. If cooking in water cannot be avoided, use as little water as possible and reuse that same water in a soup or stock gravy.
3. Keep food wrapped to prevent oxidation.
4. If appropriate, keep foods cool to decrease the activity of enzymes.
5. Do not add baking soda to green vegetables to give them a bright green color.
6. Store foods in the dark or in opaque containers.
7. Cut foods into medium-size pieces for cooking. Large pieces usually cook too slowly, and very small pieces promote oxidation and loss of vitamins into the cooking water.

8. Avoid holding food at serving temperature for a prolonged period of time, such as on a steam table. This procedure not only increases vitamin loss, but also affects texture and increases the risk of food poisoning.

As compared to vitamins, minerals are relatively indestructible, although they can be lost in the cooking water and drippings from roasted or broiled meats. Precautions such as reusing the cooking water and the defatted drippings can help retain the mineral content.

The fiber content of a meal can be raised by using high-fiber ingredients and by not removing the peel from some fruits and vegetables. Serving whole-grain breads and rolls, incorporating legumes into the menu, and using unpeeled potatoes in soups and stews are just a few ways in which you can increase a meal's fiber level.

Lowering the fat content of a food can usually be achieved with little change in flavor. Simply decreasing the amount of butter, margarine, or oil for sautéing can greatly reduce fat and therefore calorie content. Using low-fat ingredients will have the same effect: fish, skinless poultry, lean meats, and low-fat milk products. Broiling, steaming, or poaching foods will produce a final product that is lower in fat than fried foods. Instead of using the traditional fat and flour roux for thickening, flour can be mixed with a cold liquid and heated until thickened, omitting fat completely. Chilling stocks and soups, then removing the fat that has hardened on top, is also an effective way to decrease fat calories.

When fat levels are lowered in a food, cholesterol is often reduced at the same time. One of the most common high-cholesterol ingredients used in many foods is egg yolk. It is often effective to substitute two egg whites for one whole egg or to use a cholesterol-free egg substitute. Decreasing saturated fat in foods and raising the proportion of unsaturated fat may help to reduce blood cholesterol levels. This process can be achieved by using liquid oils instead of solid fats; in particular, most animal fats should be avoided, as well as highly saturated vegetable fats such as coconut and palm oils.

Salt is an expendable item in most recipes; herbs and spices can be used to enhance the lost flavor. Cooking with fresh or frozen ingredients is preferable, as most canned foods contain high levels of sodium.

Replacing rich, sugary desserts with fresh fruits and lighter, low-fat choices on a menu will help patrons lower their sugar and calorie intake. While dessert is often an opportunity to indulge, a delicious fruit sorbet or light soufflé can be satisfying without providing a high-sugar and high-calorie intake. Reducing the amount of sugar in a recipe often requires experimentation. Adding chopped fruit, extra spices, and extracts can compensate for the loss of sweetness.

Conclusions

Nutritious foods can be incorporated into almost every menu. The benefit to the consumer is the possibility of enjoying better health. It is also profitable for the foodservice operation to modify its menu and make it more attractive for a wider variety of patrons.

 ## Review Questions

1. What are the six groups of nutrients that provide a nutritious diet?

2. How can the Five Basic Food Groups Plan help to provide a nutritious diet?

3. Which groups of people are likely to be deficient in nutrients?

4. Which dietary changes can help prevent heart disease?

5. How can a foodservice operation offer more nutritious foods to its customers?

 ## Additional Readings

Karen Eich Drummond and Lisa M. Brefere, *Nutrition for the Foodservice Professional*, 4th ed. (New York: John Wiley & Sons, 2001).

Mary B. Grosvenor and Lori A. Smolin, *Nutrition Science and Application*, 2nd ed. (Fort Worth, TX: Saunders College Publishing, 1994).

Sandy Kapoor, *Professional Healthy Cooking*. (New York: John Wiley & Sons, 1995).

Frances Sizer and Eleanor Whitney, *Nutrition Concepts and Controversies*, 7th ed. (Belmont, CA: Wadsworth Publishing Co., 1997).

 ## Acknowledgment

This chapter was contributed by Jennifer Schlitzer, M.S., R.D.

Chapter 4

Foodservice Menus

A **menu** is a list of food and beverage items. In order to plan a successful menu, a foodservice professional must first identify the style of menu to be used. There are three styles of menus: *à la carte, semi à la carte, and prix fixe.* Once the style of menu has been selected, a study of the foodservice characteristics of the menu must be examined.

The **foodservice characteristics** of a menu are broken down into eight elements: type of menu, food availability, equipment, expense level, atmosphere, proficiency, customer makeup, and type of service. These elements can be applied to any menu. Identification and understanding of the foodservice characteristics of a menu are vital to a general understanding of menu planning within the foodservice industry.

 *Objectives*

1. To define the three styles of menus: à la carte, semi à la carte, and prix fixe
2. To provide the student with an explanation of the foodservice characteristics as they relate to the menus presented

3. To define American, French, and Russian service

4. To explain and discuss how the foodservice characteristics of a menu apply to various foodservice menus

Menu Styles

In the foodservice industry, there are three styles of menus: the à la carte menu, the semi à la carte menu, and the prix fixe menu.

The **à la carte menu**—Everything on the menu is priced separately, from appetizers to desserts.

The **semi à la carte menu**—A menu in this category usually prices appetizers, soups, and desserts separately. The entrée usually will include a salad, potato, vegetable, and sometimes a beverage. This style of menu is the most popular today.

The **prix fixe menu**—This type of menu offers a complete meal at a set price.

Foodservice Characteristics

The eight foodservice characteristics of a menu are*:

1. Type of menu
2. Food availability
3. Equipment
4. Expense level
5. Atmosphere
6. Proficiency
7. Customer makeup
8. Type of service

*The authors wish to express their thanks to Lothar A. Kreck, author of *Menus: Analysis and Planning,* 2nd ed., 1984, for the outline of the foodservice characteristics of menus.

Summer

Appetizers

Cantaloupe Melon *
half a melon filled with mixed berries and Muscat Beaune de Venise
17.00

Chilled Spicy Calamari *
pan fried calamari, served chilled with red pepper, onion and black olive
18.00

Watermelon and Goat Cheese Compression
layers of watermelon and goat cheese, sprinkled with black pepper, olive oil and chives
16.00

"Brandade" of Cod Salad
mousse of salted cod and mild spices, served with Virginia mesclun greens and crispy croutons
15.00

Marinated Diver Scallops *
Diver scallops marinated in fine herbs, served with summer truffles
18.00

Mille Feuilles of Foie Gras
Hudson Valley foie gras layered in between puff pastry, drizzled with light sweet and sour sauce
24.00

Grilled Fennel *
grilled baby fennel tossed with lemon garlic and extra virgin olive oil
17.00

Tuna Tapenade *
raw sushi-grade yellow fin tuna, served with a Provence "Tapenade" paste
of capers, anchovies, olives and lemon juice
20.00

Soups

Chilled Lobster Gazpacho
light and spicy summer soup, made with puree of tomatoes and steamed loister
16.00

Vichyssoise with Ossetra Caviar
creamy potato and leek soup, served chilled and topped with Ossetra caviar
19.00

Vegetarian Entree

Gratin of Coquillette
tiny coquillette pasta shells, tossed with summer truffles, extra virgin olive oil and grated Reggiano-parmesan
24.00

* Spa Cuisine - Chef Madani has created these lighter dishes to be lower in fat, cholestoral and sodium.

FIGURE 4-1 À la carte Menu. *(Courtesy of the Willard Intercontinental, Washington, D.C.)*

Menu

Fish and Shellfish

Loup de Mer
steamed loup de mer, served with asparagus and chanterelle mushroom risotto
30.00

Atlantic Salmon *
grilled fillet of Atlantic salmon, drizzled with an exquisite sauce of coffee and balsamic vinegar reduction
26.00

Chilean Sea Bass *
poached fillet of Chilean sea bass, served with lightly pan-fried leeks and green leek vinaigrette
27.00

John Dory *
pan-fried fillet of John Dory with green onions and pickled lemon, served in its own juice
29.00

Maine Lobster
Maine lobster sauteed in "Buerre Méniere," served with summer vegetables and a light ginger sauce
36.00

Meat and Poultry

Colorado Rack of Lamb
roasted rack of lamb, complemented with summer vegetable ratatouille and herbs compote
32.00

Veal Sweetbreads
pan-fried veal sweetbreads set atop a bed of persillade and sprinkled with a tangy lingonberry sauce
28.00

Black Angus Beef Tenderloin
grilled beef tenderloin, served with marinated pickled vegetables
30.00

Barbarie Duck Breast
roasted duck breast, seasoned with cinnamon and paprika, splashed with balsamic vinegar and passion fruit sauce
29.00

Roasted Amish Chicken (serves two)
whole roasted Amish chicken with caraway seeds, served in its own natural juices
(please allow 45 minutes preparation time)
54.00

Cheese

a selection of the finest domestic and imported cheeses are available
to follow your main course
16.00 per person

Chef Madani will be delighted to create a Chef's Tasting Menu for your enjoyment.

FIGURE 4-1 Continued.

The Pointer Boat

The Pointer Room at Stafford's Pier is literally "on the water". It was the boat house for the Harbor Point Association's taxi boat, THE POINTER, which ran between Harbor Point and the Village of Harbor Springs. Because there are no cars allowed on the Point, THE POINTER provided a vital link for the residents of the Association during the summer months. There were a total of three different vessels, all named THE POINTER, which ran from 1930 until 1962.

In May 1990, Stafford Smith, founder of Stafford's Hospitality, had the last of these gracious yachts re-launched. This completely restored POINTER is now on display outside Stafford's Pier where people used to catch the boat for service to the Harbor Point Hotel.

Using vintage photographs by Virgil Haynes, Harbor Springs boat builder, Steve Van Dam spent seven months creating an authentic restoration of THE POINTER, complete to the green-upholstered interior seating and side curtains. He added a beautifully designed compass rose table, ice storage area and sink to make the vessel a bit more yacht-like. As close as Mr. Van Dam can figure, this POINTER was a work boat built in Chessel, Michigan in 1934.

Appetizers

CRAB CAKES: Crabmeat, bell peppers and green onions served with a creamy Dijon horseradish sauce. $9.95

STUFFED PORTABELLA MUSHROOM: Filled with crab meat stuffing and baked. $9.95

SPINACH PASTA ROLL: Fresh herb pasta stuffed with spinach, cheese and root vegetables served on a roasted red pepper coulis. $6.50

COCKTAIL SHRIMP: Poached in herbs and spices and served chilled $9.95

OYSTERS ON THE HALF SHELL: The freshest Bluepoint oysters. $9.50

PIER STYLE FROG LEGS: Deep fried and tossed in garlic butter. $6.95

OYSTERS ROCKEFELLER: Baked with spinach, bacon, shallots, Parmesan and cream. $9.50

ESCARGOT: Baked with prosciutto, butter, spinach, garlic and feta cheese $6.75

BAKED ONION SOUP: Topped with parmesan and Gruyere cheeses. $4.50

Soups

SEAFOOD CHOWDER: Cream style with shrimp, scallops, clams. $3.75

SOUP OF THE DAY: Freshly made from our original recipes. $3.25

GAZPACHO: A south-of-the-border Summer tradition. $3.75

CHILLED CHERRY SOUP: Made with Michigan sweet and tart cherries, yogurt, rum and brandy. $3.75

Salads

SPINACH SALAD: Baby spinach, mushrooms and croutons tossed with lemon, garlic and olive oil.

RASPBERRY VINAIGRETTE: Our house salad of bibb lettuce, walnuts, mushrooms, dried cherries and scallions, topped with creamy raspberry vinaigrette dressing.

BAKED FETA CHEESE: Bibb and radicchio lettuces, lentils, scallions and smoked bacon tossed in balsamic vinaigrette dressing, topped with warmed feta cheese.

CAESAR: Crisp romaine, parmesan cheese, garlic croutons and anchovies tossed with Stafford's Caesar dressing.

SLICED TOMATO SALAD: With roasted garlic and basil vinaigrette, presented atop mixed greens with feta cheese.

Please: no smoking of pipes or cigars in the dining room

5-99

FIGURE 4-2 Semi à la carte Menu. *(Courtesy of the Pointer Room at Stafford's Pier, Harbor Springs, MI.)*

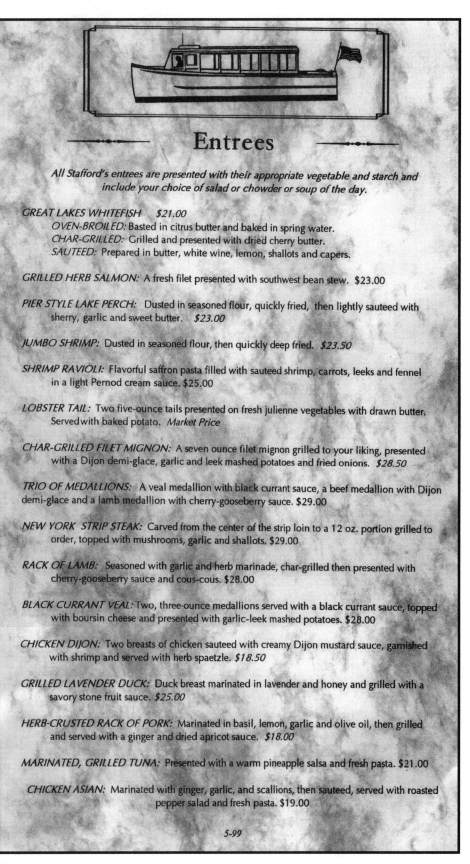

Entrees

All Stafford's entrees are presented with their appropriate vegetable and starch and include your choice of salad or chowder or soup of the day.

GREAT LAKES WHITEFISH $21.00
OVEN-BROILED: Basted in citrus butter and baked in spring water.
CHAR-GRILLED: Grilled and presented with dried cherry butter.
SAUTEED: Prepared in butter, white wine, lemon, shallots and capers.

GRILLED HERB SALMON: A fresh filet presented with southwest bean stew. $23.00

PIER STYLE LAKE PERCH: Dusted in seasoned flour, quickly fried, then lightly sauteed with sherry, garlic and sweet butter. $23.00

JUMBO SHRIMP: Dusted in seasoned flour, then quickly deep fried. $23.50

SHRIMP RAVIOLI: Flavorful saffron pasta filled with sauteed shrimp, carrots, leeks and fennel in a light Pernod cream sauce. $25.00

LOBSTER TAIL: Two five-ounce tails presented on fresh julienne vegetables with drawn butter. Served with baked potato. *Market Price*

CHAR-GRILLED FILET MIGNON: A seven ounce filet mignon grilled to your liking, presented with a Dijon demi-glace, garlic and leek mashed potatoes and fried onions. $28.50

TRIO OF MEDALLIONS: A veal medallion with black currant sauce, a beef medallion with Dijon demi-glace and a lamb medallion with cherry-gooseberry sauce. $29.00

NEW YORK STRIP STEAK: Carved from the center of the strip loin to a 12 oz. portion grilled to order, topped with mushrooms, garlic and shallots. $29.00

RACK OF LAMB: Seasoned with garlic and herb marinade, char-grilled then presented with cherry-gooseberry sauce and cous-cous. $28.00

BLACK CURRANT VEAL: Two, three-ounce medallions served with a black currant sauce, topped with boursin cheese and presented with garlic-leek mashed potatoes. $28.00

CHICKEN DIJON: Two breasts of chicken sauteed with creamy Dijon mustard sauce, garnished with shrimp and served with herb spaetzle. $18.50

GRILLED LAVENDER DUCK: Duck breast marinated in lavender and honey and grilled with a savory stone fruit sauce. $25.00

HERB-CRUSTED RACK OF PORK: Marinated in basil, lemon, garlic and olive oil, then grilled and served with a ginger and dried apricot sauce. $18.00

MARINATED, GRILLED TUNA: Presented with a warm pineapple salsa and fresh pasta. $21.00

CHICKEN ASIAN: Marinated with ginger, garlic, and scallions, then sauteed, served with roasted pepper salad and fresh pasta. $19.00

5-99

FIGURE 4-2 Continued.

Chef Allen's

Sample Menu
$52.00 per person

First Course

Bahamian Lobster and Crab Cakes with Tropical Fruit Chutney
or
Open Face Ravioli with Shiitake Mushroom and Baby Spinach

Salad

Romaine Leaves with Reggiano Parmesan and Garlic Croutons
or
Field Greens with a Citrus-Hearts of Palm Vinaigrette & Spiced Pecans

Entrees

Pan Roasted Mahi Mahi with Horseradish Mashed Potato
or
Mesquite Grilled Filet Mignon with Roast Potato and Goat Cheese Hash
or
Jumbo Shrimp with Caramelized Red Onions,
Wild Mushrooms, Asparagus and Orecchiette Pasta

Dessert

Banana Rum Strudel with Caramel Flan
or
Mango, Passion Fruit and Campari Grapefruit Sorbet
in Crisp Almond Shell

19088 N.E. 29th Avenue   (305) 935-2900   Aventura, Florida 33180

FIGURE 4-3 Prix Fixe Menu. *(Courtesy of Chef Allen's, Adventura, FL.)*

Chef Allen's
Sample Menu
$64.00 per person

First Course

Rock Shrimp Hash with Roasted Corn, Crisp Bonito & Mango Ketchup
or
Grilled Portobello Mushroom with Plantain FuFu and Cilantro Pesto

Salad

Organically Grown Arugula, Belgium Endive, Toasted Pine Nuts
and Aged Sherry Vinaigrette
or
Red Heirloom Tomato Salad
with Feta and Roast Shallot Vinaigrette

Entree

Pistachio Crusted Grouper
with Rock Shrimp, Leeks, Mango and Coconut Rum
or
Tamarind Chili Roasted Duck with Wild Rice and Brazilian Peanut Salsa
or
Dijon Crusted Rack of Lamb
with Wild Mushroom Timbale, Asparagus and Truffle Butter

Dessert

Frozen Valencia Orange Soufflé with Shaved Chocolate
or
Green Apple Tart Tatin with Cinnamon Ice Cream

***** ***** *****

Chocolate Truffles & Butter Cookies

19088 N.E. 29th Avenue   (305) 935-2900   Aventura, Florida 33180

FIGURE 4-3 Continued.

NEW WORLD CUISINE

Chef Allen's
Sample Menu
$75.00 per person

First Course

Lobster Martini with Purple Potato, Red Peppers and Yellow Tomato
or
Jumbo Crab Meat Napoleon with Osetra Caviar

Salad

Organically Grown Arugula Salad with Pistachio Crusted Goat Cheese
or
Exotic Greens, Herbs, Nuts and Berries

Entrees

Tribeca Veal Chop with a Calabaza & Almond Risotto,
Double Mustard and Wild Mushroom Ragout
or
Pan Roasted Pompano
with Saffron Mashed Potato and Truffled Tomato Bisque
or
Grilled Rack of Shrimp
with Fennel, Black Olive Cous Cous and Preserved Lemon

Dessert

White Chocolate Macadamia Nut Mousse Bombe
or
Grand Marnier and Raspberry Soufflé

**** **** **** ****

"Cigar Box" of Handmade Chocolates, Truffles and Cookies

19088 N.E. 29th Avenue   (305) 935-2900   Aventura, Florida 33180

FIGURE 4-3 Continued.

In the following discussion of the 10 different types of menus, we will discuss each of the foodservice characteristics listed above. These menus include

- Breakfast menus
- Luncheon menus
- Dinner menus
- Special occasion menus
- Institutional menus
- Room service menus
- Ethnic menus
- Specialty menus
- Wine menus
- Dessert menus

Breakfast Menus

Type of Menu. Most breakfast menus contain both à la carte and semi à la carte sections. The à la carte section offers juices, fruits, cereals, eggs, meats, bakery goods, and sometimes beverages. The semi à la carte section offers a wide variety of combinations (for example, two eggs any style with bacon or sausage served with toast, or three pancakes with syrup and bacon or sausage served with home fries).

Food Availability. Food for the breakfast menu usually can be purchased from local purveyors. Items should be taken off the menu if they are not easily available or if they don't sell.

Equipment. When planning a breakfast menu, you must pay careful attention to the purchasing and the placing of equipment. The equipment usually consists of a broiler or grill, flat-top range or open burner, griddle, convection oven, plate warmers, toasters, and microwave ovens.

Equipment should be located in a logical and compact fashion to aid employees in cooking and serving food promptly. The most common complaint of breakfast customers is that they are served lukewarm food that should be served hot.

Expense Level. The prices of food items on a breakfast menu are low to moderate, since most people do not expect to pay much for breakfast. However, large hotels can and often do charge more than other foodservice establishments for this meal.

Atmosphere. A breakfast menu should reflect the decor of the operation. For example, if the tablecloth, carpeting, and napkins are white and the flowers on the tables are yellow, the menu should be light in color.

Proficiency. All breakfast items are generally cooked to order. Cooks must be quick and well organized. One does not need to be a master chef to prepare items on a breakfast menu. The service personnel also have to be quick and efficient because of the high turnover rate during the breakfast service.

Customer Makeup. Breakfast customers are often in a hurry because they are either on their way to work or returning home after working a third shift.

Type of Service. Breakfast service, for the most part, is American. One waitstaff person takes the order and brings it to the table. The table is then cleaned by a dining room attendant.

Type of Menu. The menu (Figure 4-4) is a combination of à la carte and prix fixe menu. The beverages, appetizers, entrées, and desserts are à la carte. The prix fixe section includes three courses: appetizer, entrée, and dessert. Most of the items are served hot, such as appetizers, egg dishes, crêpes, steak, trout, and desserts.

Food Availability. The breakfast items are obtained through local purveyors.

Equipment. A flat-top range or open burner is needed for soups, poached eggs, and sautéed items. Refrigeration is required to store dairy products, juices, meats, fish, fruits, and vegetables. A griddle or a tilting skillet is needed for meats and egg dishes. Crêpes Fitzgerald and other such desserts are cooked on a heating unit called a *réchaud* with the use of a *guéridon*, or cart, prepared and served table-side.

Expense Level. Menu prices at Brennan's might be considered high, but in a city where dining out can be an expensive proposition, Brennan's reputation for quality food and service can demand their prices. The prices range from $5 for a Mimosa to $36 for the Steak and Eggs Brennan.

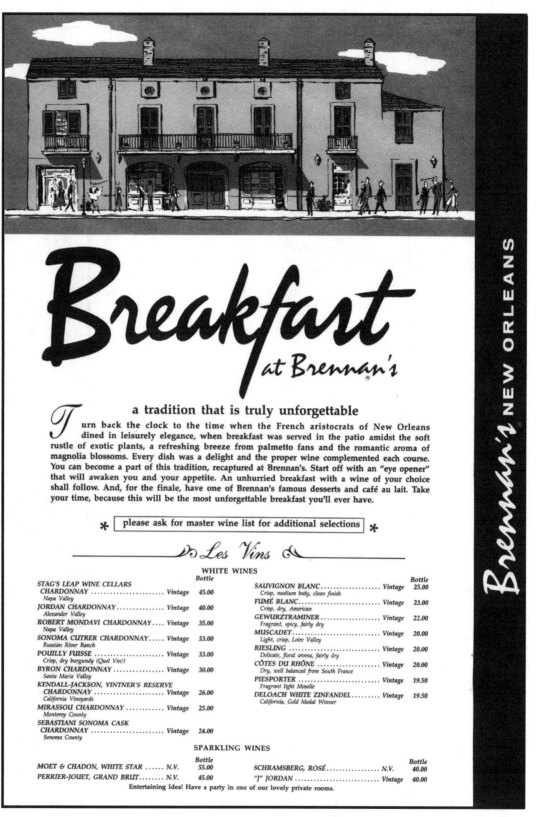

FIGURE 4-4 Breakfast Menu. *(Courtesy of Brennan's, New Orleans, LA.)*

Breakfast at Brennan's AND DINNER, TOO
— our most recent cookbook and the story of our legacy —
to purchase, ask your waiter or the bartender for information

Eye Openers

To sharpen your taste as well as your appetite

ABSINTHE SUISSESSE 5.00
*An old New Orleans drink revived by our founder for your enjoyment.
Guaranteed to put you in the mood for this carefree old city.*

SAZERAC 5.00
*The Sazerac is a New Orleans drink made with bourbon and a little mystery.
The glass is first coated with absinthe to give the Sazerac its special taste.*

OJEN FRAPPÉ 5.00
*Just as in the days of the old coffee shops, there are those who prefer Ojen,
the absinthe of the Spanish aristocracy.*

CREOLE BLOODY MARY 5.00

BRANDY MILK PUNCH 5.00

ABSINTHE FRAPPÉ 5.00

NEW ORLEANS GIN FIZZ 5.00

BULL SHOT 5.00
Vodka, beef bouillon, Worcestershire.

BLOODY BULL 5.00
Vodka, beef bouillon, Worcestershire, tomato juice.

MIMOSA 5.00
Champagne and orange juice

CHABLIS CASSIS (KIR) 5.00

KIR ROYALE 5.00
Champagne with a touch of Creme de Cassis

RED ROOSTER 5.00
*Vodka, orange juice and cranberry juice. . .makes you want to stand up and
crow!*

MR. FUNK OF NEW ORLEANS 5.00
*Named for our late Cellar Master. A delightful combination
of champagne, cranberry juice and peach schnapps.*

Mineral Waters

EVIAN (FRANCE)   SAN PELLEGRINO (ITALY)
1 liter   1 liter
6.95

Appetizers

Secret herbs and spices make these delightful tempters

OYSTER SOUP BRENNAN 7.75	SOUTHERN BAKED APPLE WITH DOUBLE CREAM 6.50
CREOLE ONION SOUP 7.25	BERRIES IN SEASON WITH DOUBLE CREAM 6.50
BANANA SLICES WITH DOUBLE CREAM 5.00	NEW ORLEANS TURTLE SOUP A Brennan Specialty 7.75

Omelettes-Oeufs

Country fresh eggs prepared in a very sophisicated manner

CHEDDAR CHEESE AND HAM OMELETTE 15.75
FRESH MUSHROOM OMELETTE 15.75
OMELETTE FLORENTINE 15.75
With creamed spinach
CAJUN TASSO OMELETTE WITH CHEDDAR CHEESE 16.95
Cajun smoked spicy ham. A new experience!
CAJUN GRILLED ANDOUILLE OMELETTE WITH CHEDDAR CHEESE 16.95
Spicy cajun sausage. "Nothing like it!"
CRABMEAT OMELETTE 18.75
Topped with Hollandaise sauce.
CRAWFISH OMELETTE (seasonal) 18.75
Topped with Hollandaise sauce.

We suggest a bottle of Muscadet to
complement any of the above entrees,
$20.00

AND HERE IS A TRADITIONAL BRENNAN BREAKFAST:
*This is the way it was done in leisurely antebellum days. . .First, Oyster
Soup Brennan, then an Egg Benedict, followed by a hearty Ribeye with
fresh mushrooms and Hot French Bread. For the finale — Bananas Foster.
Quel delice mon ami!*
$50.00
Suggested Eye Opener - Absinthe Suissesse $5.00
Suggested Wine — Perrier-Jouet, Grand Brut $45.00

Due to certain conditions we sometimes
substitute fresh crawfish tails for lump crabmeat.

Table d'hote P

Three Course P

APPET
Choice

Southern Baked App
Berries in Season
Creole Onion Soup
New Orleans Turt

ENT

EGGS SARDOU
*Poached eggs on artichoke bottoms n
covered with Hollandaise sauce.*
Suggested Wine — Fumé Blanc $23.0

EGGS BAYOU LAFOURCHE
*Poached eggs atop andouille Cajun sa
Hollandaise sauce.*
Suggested Wine — Gewurztraminer $

EGGS BENEDICT
*A traditional dish of poached eggs at
topped with Hollandaise sauce.*
Suggested Wine — Byron Chardonna

EGGS ST. CHARLES
Poached eggs atop delicately fried trout
Suggested Wine — Fumé Blanc $23.0

EGGS HUSSARDE .... A Brennan's
*One of the dishes that put "Bre
Poached eggs atop Holland rusks, Cana
Topped with Hollandaise sauce.*
Suggested Wine — Sauvignon Blanc

OYSTERS BENEDICT
*Fresh Gulf oysters fried to perfection
Hollandaise sauce.*
Suggested Wine — Gewurztraminer $

SHRIMP SARDOU
*Deliciously spicy fried shrimp atop slic
creamed spinach and covered with Holla*
Suggested Wine — Sauvignon Blanc

EGGS ELLEN
Grilled filet of salmon topped with poach
Suggested Wine — Gewurztraminer $

EGGS OWEN
*We start with a fine beef hash, then add
Vin sauce.*
Suggested Wine — Piesporter $19.50

EGGS SHANNON
*Poached eggs atop fried trout, served
with Hollandaise sauce.*
Suggested Wine — Sonoma Cutrer C

EGGS PORTUGUESE
*Flaky pastry shells filled with freshly
parsley and shallots. Topped with poa
sauce.*
Suggested Wine — Robert Mondavi C

EGGS NOUVELLE ORLÉANS
*Poached eggs served on a bed of lump
sauce.*
Suggested Wine — Sauvignon Blanc

DES
Choi

BANANA
A Brennan Creation a
Bananas sauted in butter, brown
then flamed in rum. Ser
Scandalous

CREPES FITZGERAL
Crepes filled with a delicate filli
served with a topping of strawberries flam

CREOLE CHOCOL
A Chocolat

A Typical Cr

EGG S
Poached egg on artichoke bottom nestled
with Holla

GRILLADES
Sauted baby veal served in a divinely
freshly ground pepper.

CREPES F
A Brennan Creation. Crepes with a deli
served with a topping of strawberrie

Suggested Wine — Pou

FIGURE 4-4 Continued.

Breakfast at Brennan's without wine is like a day without sunshine!

Viandes

Glamorous things happen to our finest meats.

GRILLED HAM STEAK, EGGS THEODORE 27.00
Scrambled eggs served with a banana sauteed in butter, cinnamon and brown sugar.
Suggested Wine — Riesling $20.00 / Bottle

GRILLED HAM STEAK.. 25.75
Suggested Wine — Sonoma Cutrer Chardonnay $33.00 / Bottle

GRILLED HAM STEAK ROYALE 27.00
Covered with two poached eggs and Hollandaise sauce.
Suggested Wine — Byron Chardonnay $30.00 / Bottle

RIBEYE STEAK 35.00
A prime 14oz. ribeye, grilled to your liking in its natural juices.
Suggested Wine — Sebastiani Sonoma Cask Cabernet Sauvignon $27.00 / Bottle

STEAK AND EGGS BRENNAN.................................. 36.00
A prime 14oz. ribeye, grilled to your taste, topped with poached eggs and Hollandaise sauce.
Suggested Wine — Zinfandel $30.00 / Bottle

GRILLADES AND GRITS 35.00
Sauteed baby veal served in a divinely seasoned Creole sauce with fine herbs and freshly ground pepper. A New Orleans Delight!
Suggested Wine — Pouilly Fuisse $33.00 / Bottle

VEAL SHAWN... 34.50
Sauteed baby veal topped with poached eggs and Hollandaise sauce.
Suggested Wine — Jordan Chardonnay $40.00 / Bottle

VEAL 417 .... 34.50
Sauteed baby veal topped with lump crabmeat and Hollandaise sauce.
Suggested Wine — Jordan Chardonnay $40.00 / Bottle

VEAL PECAN 34.50
Sauteed veal topped with crabmeat, roasted pecans and pecan butter.
Suggested Wine — Sonoma Cutrer Chardonnay $33.00 / Bottle

Poissons

OYSTERS ROCKEFELLER (15 min.)............................ 11.50
Brennan's special treatment of this world famous sauce.

ESCARGOTS BORDELAISE (15 min)................ Half Dozen 11.50
Suggested Wine — Muscadet $20.00 / Bottle

BRENNAN'S BLACKENED REDFISH 30.50
Brennan's version of blackened redfish grilled to perfection with Brennan's own seasonings.
Suggested Wine — Pouilly Fuisse $33.00 / Bottle

TROUT NANCY 29.50
Filet of trout sauteed and topped with lump crabmeat sprinkled with capers, lemon butter sauce.
Suggested Wine — Robert Mondavi Chardonnay $35.00 / Bottle

TROUT PECAN.. 27.00
Filet of fresh trout sauteed and topped with roasted pecans and pecan butter.
Suggested Wine — Sonoma Cutrer Chardonnay $33.00 / Bottle

Desserts

For these unbelievable creations - diets be damned!

BANANAS FOSTER .. A Brennan Creation and now World Famous! 7.25
Bananas sauteed in butter, brown sugar, cinnamon and banana liqueur, then flamed in rum. Served over vanilla ice cream. Scandalously Delicious!

CREPES FITZGERALD (A Brennan Creation) 7.25
Crepes filled with a delicate filling of cream cheese and sour cream served with a topping of strawberries flamed in Maraschino. Scrumptious!

CREOLE CHOCOLATE SUICIDE CAKE 6.00
A Chocoholic's Fantasy!

BRENNAN'S IRISH COFFEE 6.95

A Typical New Orleans Breakfast

Start with an Eye Opener
Brandy Milk Punch or Creole Bloody Mary $5.00
SOUTHERN BAKED APPLE WITH DOUBLE CREAM
EGGS HUSSARDE......A Brennan's Original!
One of the dishes that put "Breakfast at Brennan's" on the map.
Poached eggs atop Holland rusks, Canadian bacon and Marchand de Vin sauce.
Topped with Hollandaise sauce.
BRENNAN'S HOT FRENCH BREAD
BANANAS FOSTER
A Brennan Creation and now World Famous
Bananas sauteed in butter, brown sugar, cinnamon and banana liqueur then flamed in rum. Served over vanilla Ice Cream.
$35.00
It's traditional to have wine with breakfast at Brennan's — we recommend
Pouilly Fuisse
$33.00 / Bottle

Not responsible for loss or exchange of wearing apparel or personal property.

Due to certain conditions we sometimes substitute other fresh gulf or farm raised fish for redfish or trout.

FIGURE 4-4 Continued.

Atmosphere. The multicolored menu composed of both bright and pastel colors, reflects the bold and exciting flavors found in New Orleans cuisine as well as the sophistication of a more leisurely time. The style of print is refined and elegant. Menu offerings are extensive and diversified.

Proficiency. Employees in both the front of the house and the back of the house are required to have extensive product knowledge. Chefs also must be familiar with a variety of cooking techniques, such as baking, grilling, poaching, and sautéing. The waitstaff must be familiar with item preparation and is expected to prepare some table-side items, such as Bananas Foster.

Customer Makeup. Customers consist of tourists, business people, and couples sometimes celebrating special occasions.

Type of Service. The type of service is American and French.

Luncheon Menus

Type of Menu. A luncheon menu can be à la carte or semi à la carte. À la carte items include appetizers, salads, cold and hot sandwiches, entrées, desserts, and beverages. The semi à la carte section includes entrées with salad, vegetable, and potato. Many luncheon menus offer daily specials as well. Specials are usually presented in the following ways:

1. On a blackboard at the entrance of the restaurant
2. Inside the menu as a clip-on
3. Verbally by the waitstaff person

Food Availability. Food supplies for a luncheon menu can be obtained through local purveyors. If a food item is difficult to obtain but is popular, it should be offered as a special when available.

Equipment. Baked, barbecued, braised, broiled, fried, grilled, poached, roasted, sautéed, simmered, smoked, and steamed items on the luncheon menu require a full range of equipment. The specific equipment needed for lunch preparation will depend on the menu items offered.

Expense Level. Prices on a luncheon menu will depend on the menu items, the type of operation, and the location of the establishment. The prices can range from low to high.

Atmosphere. The luncheon menu should reflect the decor of the operation. In a seafood restaurant, for example, the tablecloths might be light blue with white napkins. The menu cover might be light blue with a dark blue anchor on the cover, symbolizing the logo or design of the restaurant. The inside might be light blue with dark blue print to match the cover.

Proficiency. Preparing and serving a luncheon menu requires professional cooks and waitstaff. Luncheon items such as appetizers, soups, entrées, and desserts are frequently made from scratch and require preparation by someone who has a culinary background. The waitstaff also should have some culinary knowledge so that they can describe specials and other dishes in detail to customers.

Customer Makeup. The clientele is all-encompassing, consisting of business people, tourists, retirees, and so forth.

Type of Service. Luncheon service is most frequently American service—quick and efficient. Many people have limited time for lunch, and they expect fast service as well as good food.

Type of Menu. This style of menu is a combination of semi à la carte and à la carte (Figure 4-5). The entrées and sandwiches come with traditional accoutrements. Appetizers and salads are à la carte. Marché has a variety of sandwiches as well, which is characteristic of a luncheon menu.

Food Availability. Food items are procured from local purveyors.

Equipment. Soups, pasta, and sautéed chicken breast require a flat-top range or open burner. A grill or broiler is needed for Yellowfin Tuna Niçoise, and the Grilled Sliced Steak. The Oven-roasted Tomatoes and the Baked Giant Shrimp require an oven.

Expense Level. The expense level is moderate. Marché's Ceasar Salad is $7, and the Baked Giant Shrimp is $17.

Atmosphere. The menu reflects the overall decor and style of the restaurant.

Proficiency. The waitstaff must be knowledgeable about the preparation of items such as Smoked Duck Breast and Herb-Crusted Whitefish. The chefs are required to know a variety of cooking techniques,

Diane M. Halle Library
ENDICOTT COLLEGE
Beverly, MA 01915

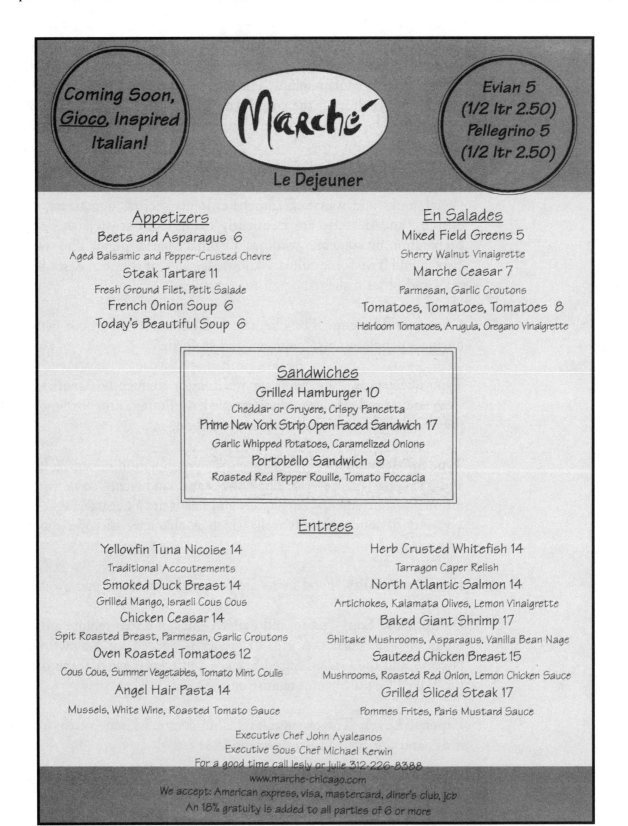

FIGURE 4-5 Luncheon Menu. *(Courtesy of Marché, Chicago, IL.)*

such as baking, broiling, grilling, roasting, sautéing, and simmering. Knowledge of sauces is also needed for Tomato Mint Coulis, Roasted Tomato Sauce, and Lemon Chicken Sauce.

Customer Makeup. Business people, tourists, couples, and local merchants are the customers.

Type of Service. The type of service is American.

Dinner Menus

Type of Menu. A dinner menu is usually a combination of both à la carte items and semi à la carte items. The dinner menu has more appetizers and entrées than a luncheon menu. The dinner menu is often the most expensive type of menu.

Food Availability. Most supplies are not difficult to obtain. Items that are too difficult to obtain should be eliminated from the menu.

Equipment. The menu determines the equipment needed to produce items effectively and efficiently. For example, a specialty restaurant featuring steak and seafood items needs broilers or a grill, deep-fat fryers, steamers, steam kettles, ovens, and flat-top ranges for sautéing.

Expense Level. Pricing will depend upon the type of restaurant and the items featured on the menu. Dinner items are usually more expensively priced than luncheon and breakfast offerings.

Atmosphere. The menu should reflect the decor. A French restaurant might have red carpeting, gold napkins, and red tablecloths. The menu cover could be red with the name of the restaurant in gold print. The inside of the menu could have a light gold background and red print.

Proficiency. The food items on the menu, again, will determine the degree of skill needed by the staff. Dinner offerings might list Baked Ham, which is usually served with a sauce. Sauces require a skilled kitchen staff. The waitstaff should also be aware of preparation methods so that they can answer guests' questions.

Customer Makeup. The clientele may be couples or families celebrating special events, or working persons who come to enjoy a leisurely meal.

Type of Service. The type of service can range from American to French to Russian. In **American service,** there is one waitstaff person who takes the order and brings it to the table. The table is then cleared and reset by a dining room attendant.

French service requires two waiters: a captain and a secondary waiter. The captain takes the order, does the table-side cooking, and brings the drinks, appetizers, entrées, and desserts to the table. The secondary waiter brings the bread and water, clears each course, crumbs the table, and serves the coffee.

In **Russian service,** the entrée, vegetables, and potatoes are served from a platter onto a plate. In modified Russian service, which is sometimes used in seafood or specialty houses, the waitstaff person serves the entrée from a casserole using a serving spoon and a fork.

Type of Menu. This style of menu (Figure 4-6) is a prix fixe menu. The cost of the meal includes a first course selection, between course selection, main course selection, and a choice of desserts. Dinner might consist of the Carpaccio of Baby Lamb with Rosemary Mustard; Endive and Watercress Salad with Walnuts, Pears, Bacon and Maytag Blue Cheese; Pan Seared Tenderloin of Veal with Chanterelles, English Peas and Raviolis of Virginia Country Ham and Fontina Cheese; and a Caramelized Banana Tart with Roasted Banana Ice Cream. The menu also offers a large variety of after-dinner drinks. A prix fixe vegetarian menu is available for guests who are health conscious.

Food Availability. This menu calls for at least one purveyor who specializes in high-quality gourmet foods because of such items on the menu as Pan Seared Chilean Sea Bass with Shallots Three Ways, Fava Beans, Fingerling Potatoes, Wild Mushrooms and Red Wine Demi Glace. Other food items can be obtained through local purveyors.

Equipment. The preparation of Roasted Eggplant Raviolis with Medallions of Lobster in a Tomato Basil Butter Sauce requires a flattop range or open burner. The Grilled Tenderloin of Beef with Bone Marrow Gratin on Roesti Potatoes, with Summer Truffles requires the use of a grill or a broiler. The Local Rabbit Braised in Apple Cider with Wild Mushrooms and Garlic Mashed Potatoes requires an oven.

Expense Level. The price level is high. The cost of the prix fixe four-course dinner is $128 per person.

Atmosphere. The menu cover in cream and gold reflects the grace and sophistication of The Inn at Little Washington. An extensive selection

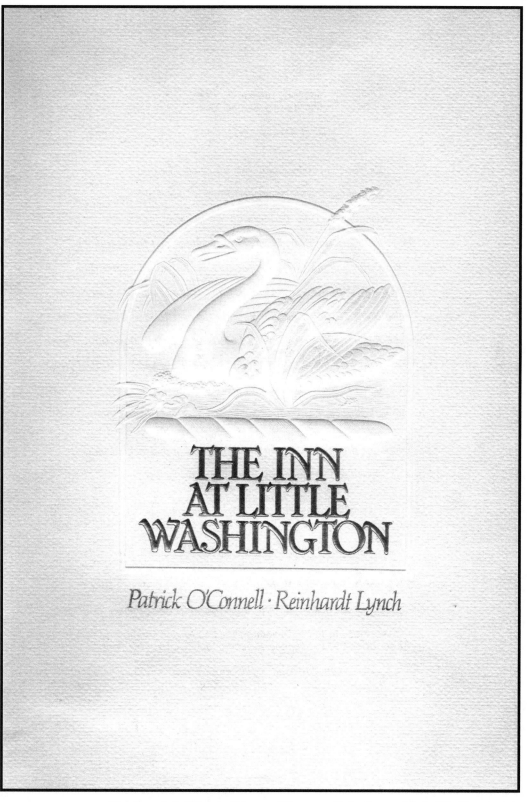

FIGURE 4-6 Dinner Menu. *(Courtesy of the Inn at Little Washington, Washington, VA.)*

Saturday, August 28, 1999
Our Twenty Second Year

First Course Selections

Carpaccio of Baby Lamb with Rosemary Mustard

Seared Quail with Huckleberries on a Corn Cake

Oriental-Style Tuna Tartare with Wasabi Mayonnaise

A Mélange of Prosciutto, Pear, Parmigiano-Reggiano and Baby Arugula

Porcini Pizza with Fontina Cheese, Asparagus and Virginia Country Ham

Crispy Seared Rockfish on Braised Baby Bok Choy with a Sweet and Sour Sauce

Chilled, Grilled Black Mission Figs with Virginia Country Ham and Lime Cream

Roasted Eggplant Raviolis with Medallions of Lobster in a Tomato Basil Butter Sauce

Seared Duck Foie Gras on Polenta with Virginia Country Ham and Local Blackberries

Chilled, Herb Crusted Poached Salmon with Marinated Cucumbers and Pea Puree

Risotto with Shrimp, Corn, Chanterelles and Virginia Country Ham

Our Homemade Boudin Blanc (White Sausage)
on Sauerkraut Braised in Virginia Riesling, with Fig and Apple Coulis

Chilled Crab Salad in a Tropical Fruit Coulis

A Slab of Chilled Goose Foie Gras
with Local Peaches, Pickled Cherries and Fleur de Sel

Between Course Selections

Endive and Watercress Salad with Walnuts, Pears, Bacon and Maytag Blue Cheese

A Salad of Baby Green Beans with Mustard Vinaigrette and Summer Truffles

Our Salad of Local Tomatoes with Grilled Red Onion,
Mosto Olive Oil, Parmigiano Reggiano and Toasted Pine Nuts

Lemon-Rosemary Sorbet with Vermouth

FIGURE 4-6 Continued.

Main Course Selections

Filet Mignon of Rarish Tuna Capped with Seared Duck Foie Gras
on Charred Vidalia Onions with a Burgundy Butter Sauce

Pan Seared Tenderloin of Veal with Chanterelles, English Peas
and Raviolis of Virginia Country Ham and Fontina Cheese

Pan Seared Chilean Sea Bass with Shallots Three Ways, Fava Beans,
Fingerling Potatoes, Wild Mushrooms and Red Wine Demi Glace

Grilled Tenderloin of Beef with Bone Marrow Gratin
on Roesti Potatoes, with Summer Truffles

Local Rabbit Braised in Apple Cider
with Wild Mushrooms and Garlic Mashed Potatoes

Veal Sweetbreads Braised in Ruby Port
with Clam Shell Mushrooms and Huckleberries

Barbecued Grilled Rack of Lamb in a Pecan Crust
with Sweet Potato Crisps and Corn Saute

Thrice Cooked Duck with Aromatic Asian Spices
and Peaches on Wild Rice Pecan-Pilaf

Lobster with Grapefruit, Orzo, and Citrus Butter Sauce

Choice of Dessert

One Hundred Twenty Eight Dollars Per Person
(Beverages, Tax and Gratuity Not Included)

Today's Vegetarian Selections are Available
on the Following Page

FIGURE 4-6 Continued.

e're glad you found us. We think Washington, Virginia, is a magical kind of place. Some people who come out this way find it hard to get back to where they came from.

They say the town hasn't changed much since George Washington laid it out, surveyed it and named the streets back in July of 1749. It thereby became the first Washington of all, 51 years before Washington, D.C. was established.

At about this same time in history, in Paris, France, a certain Monsieur Boulanger opened the world's first restaurant—so named because of the *restoratives*, ("restaurants")—soups and broths—that he served. While there were lodgings and hostelries where meals were served to overnight guests in existence before him, Boulanger's was the first public place where people went simply to eat a meal.

History aside, there are some things you should know about the kitchen:

Our menu changes—with the seasons, the weather, and the wind. We rewrite it frequently so there will always be a little surprise for you and a fresh new challenge for us.

Our approach to cooking, while paying homage to the lawmakers of Classical French Cuisine, reflects a belief in "the cuisine of today", healthy, eclectic, imaginative, unrestricted by ethnic boundaries and always growing.

We hope we can live up to the original meaning of our name as restaurateurs and *restore* you a little while you're here.

Thank you for giving us the opportunity.

FIGURE 4-6 Continued.

of offerings, beautifully described and elegantly prepared, provides guests with enough variety to please any palate.

Proficiency. Employees in both the front and back of the house require an extensive culinary background. Preparation of the Filet Mignon of Rarish Tuna Capped with Seared Duck Foie Gras on Charred Vidalia Onions with a Burgundy Butter Sauce requires that the chefs know how to prepare foie gras as well as Burgundy Sauce. The chefs also would have to know how to braise, bake, broil, grill, poach, and sauté to accommodate the menu items listed. Due to the complexity of the menu offerings, waitstaff would have to know in detail how each menu item is prepared.

Customer Makeup. Customers of The Inn at Little Washington consist of guests at the inn as well as dinner guests from the area who wish to celebrate special occasions in a refined and luxurious atmosphere.

Type of Service. French.

Special Occasion Menus

Type of Menu. The special occasion menu is prix fixe in style and may include alcoholic beverages. For the most part, the special occasion menu should display the theme or season on the cover of the menu, and the food items and/or garnishes should be typical of that particular season.

Food Availability. Menu planners should procure supplies early so that there are no last-minute problems.

Equipment. For the most part, the special occasion function will take place in a club or a restaurant where equipment is available. The menu planner should ensure that the equipment needed for any special items on the menu is available.

Expense Level. In some cases, entertainment is included in the price of the special menu, often making special occasion menus expensive.

Atmosphere. It is important that the menu carry the theme of the special occasion, whether it be Easter, Mother's Day, Thanksgiving, or Christmas, and so forth. Cornucopias can be displayed for Thanksgiving; spring floral bouquets, for Easter and Mother's Day; and poinsettias for Christmas.

Proficiency. Skills needed for a special occasion menu are average to high. The cooks should know in advance what will be on the menu. Organizational skills on the part of the waitstaff are necessary in order to accommodate guests who arrive at different times.

Customer Makeup. The clientele who attend special occasion functions expect good food and good service. At holiday times especially, customers can be far from home and family, and usually appreciate extra attention.

Type of Service. The style of service is usually American. The waitstaff may have to contend with the entertainment, along with setting up extra tables and chairs. As a result, the quality of food on a special occasion menu is often better than the quality of service.

Type of Menu. The style of menu (Figure 4-7) is prix fixe and offers a complete meal for one price. The menu includes a choice of soup, appetizer, salad, and entrée.

Food Availability. It is important that all food items on a special occasion menu are able to be purchased in large quantities because of the volume served. All the food items on the menu should be available through local purveyors.

Equipment. The soups and the Seafood Spring Roll with Ponzu Dipping Sauce require a flat-top range or an open burner. The Boiled or Baked Stuffed Lobster en Casserole requires a broiler or an oven. The Boneless Rack of Lamb and the Roast Tenderloin of Beef require an oven as well.

Expense Level. The expense level is high on a typical New Year's Eve menu.

Atmosphere. The menu should reflect the occasion as well as the type of establishment the restaurant wishes to portray.

Proficiency. Both the front of the house and the chefs must be fairly skilled to work a special dinner at the Stage Neck Inn. The waitstaff must have a knowledge of French service and also must be familiar with the various soups, appetizers, and entrées and their appropriate sauces. The chefs have to be skilled in all phases of cooking techniques, including baking, boiling, and roasting, as well as garde manger.

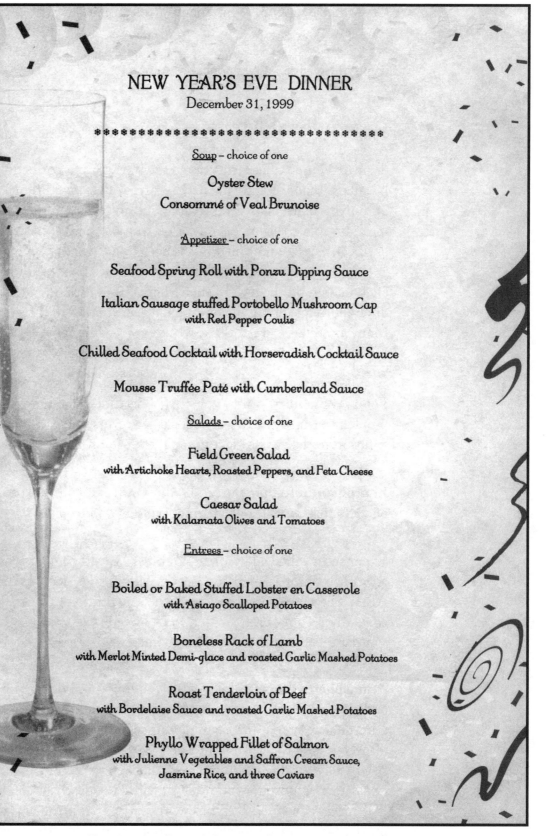

FIGURE 4-7 Special Occasion Menu. *(Courtesy of Stage Neck Inn, York Harbor, ME.)*

Customer Makeup. This menu attracts couples who are celebrating the New Year.

Type of Service. The service is French.

Institutional Menus

Type of Menu. The institutional menu is used in correctional facilities, hospitals, schools, and the armed forces. The institutional menu must be nutritionally balanced, serving the five basic food groups at each meal: bread, cereals, rice, and pasta; fruit; vegetable; meat, poultry, fish, dry beans, eggs, and nuts; milk, cheese, and yogurt.

Most institutions, especially hospitals, use a cyclical menu to alleviate boredom on the part of their clients. A cyclical menu is one that has different items on the menu each day for a period of three to five weeks. Many hospitals have a three-week cycle, while most schools and universities have a five-week cycle for their menus.

Food Availability. Procuring food does not usually present itself as a problem for institutions, since local purveyors will contract with the institution to deliver product at an agreed-upon time and frequency.

Equipment. Equipment can be difficult to obtain because of the strict budgets that institutions at times will have to follow.

Expense Level. Today, a large number of institutional food operations are run by professional foodservice companies such as ARAMARK, ARA, Service Master, and Sodexho. Institutions pay the foodservice company a sum per customer, per day. For example, a $3.50 per person/per meal amount might be charged.

Atmosphere. In many institutions, dining room decor is not a priority budget item. Administrators often see no need to improve the look of a hospital cafeteria, for example. Since patients are in the hospital out of necessity and are primarily there to get better and then leave, a consistent flow of diners is always guaranteed. Recently, however, institutions such as hospitals and health care facilities have begun to realize that nicely decorated facilities, with paintings on the walls and flowers on the tables, make meals much more enjoyable. An attractive facility also increases employee, patient, and visitor morale.

Proficiency. The chef should have a culinary background and a knowledge of special diets. The cooks can be less skilled. Most institutions encourage on-the-job training to improve the skills of their kitchen and cafeteria personnel, where safety and sanitation are a must.

Customer Makeup. The clientele is dictated by the type of institution and can range from young children in schools to senior citizens in nursing homes.

Type of Service. With the exception of food delivery to rooms in hospitals, the service is mostly cafeteria-style and self-service. Cafeteria-style service requires that many types of food be held for extended periods of time. Most hot foods are kept warm in steam tables.

Type of Menu. The institutional menu (Figure 4-8) at Forest Farm Health Care Center offers a four-week cycle menu. This menu offers the patient a nutritionally balanced meal through the use of foods from each of the five food groups.

Food Availability. Produce is acquired through local purveyors.

Equipment. Major pieces of equipment are required. Roasted Turkey and Baked Cod require the use of an oven. French toast and omelets will call for the use of a griddle. A flat-top range or open burner is required for soups, spaghetti, and pan-fried items such as the Pan-Fried Chicken Sherry. Institutional-size mixers are needed as well.

Expense Level. The cost is calculated within the overall budget in order to successfully run the operation and to generate a profit.

Atmosphere. The menu is designed to provide nutritious meals that are never boring. The cyclical menu provides the patients with variety and the reappearance of favorites as well. The meals are tastefully presented and are accompanied by seasonal specialties. Theme- and holiday-related specialties are also offered from time to time.

Proficiency. The chef needs a good culinary background and a knowledge of special diets. A registered dietician is needed for consultations regarding nutritional food value and the recommended preparation.

Customer Makeup. This menu caters to health care patients.

Type of Service. The type of service is tray service or table service.

SUNDAY	MONDAY	TUESDAY	WEDNESDAY	THURSDAY	FRIDAY	SATURDAY
ORANGE JUICE HOT/COLD CEREAL CHOICE OF EGG TOAST/MUFFIN	WEEK JUNE 14 THRU JUNE 20 JULY 12 THRU JULY 18 AUG. 9 THRU AUG.15 SEPT.6 THRU SEPT 12	DAILY ALTERNATES DINNER HAM, TURKEY, CHICKEN, MEATLOAF SUPPER CHOICE OF SOUP HAM, TURKEY, OR GRILL CHEESE SANDWICH	BREAKFAST	HS SUPPLEMENT ICE CREAM CRACKERS JUICE, SODA, MILK		
			LUNCH			
ROASTED TURKEY, STUFFING W/ GRAVY CRANBERRY SAUCE DUCHESS POTATO, GLAZED PEAS CHOCOLATE SUNDAE	VEAL CUTLET PARMESAN WITH SPAGHETTI ITALIAN GREEN BEANS SMALL SALAD STRAWBERRY CREAM PIE	MEATLOAF WITH BROWN GRAVY BAKED POTATO WITH SOUR CREAM MIXED VEGETABLE PEANUT BUTTER BROWNIE	PAN FRIED CHICKEN SHERRY WINE GRAVY MASHED POTATO STIR FRIED VEGETABLE WITH NOODLES ICE CREAM	STUFFED CABBAGE, SWEET POTATO, PEAS & CARROTS PEACH PIE	STUFFED SOLE, BAKED POTATO, GREEN BEANS WITH MUSHROOM & ONIONS CHERRY CHEESECAKE	FRANKS & BEANS BROWN BREAD, MIXED VEGETABLES BAKED APPLE
			DINNER			
CREAM OF TOMATO SOUP, TUNA SALAD ON WHEAT BREAD, PASTA SALAD, ASSORTED COOKIES	VEGETARIAN SOUP, GRILLED HAM AND CHEESE SANDWICH, DEVILED EGG, FRUITED JELLO W/ TOPPING	CORNED BEEF HASH, POACHED EGG, MIXED VEGETABLE, PEAR HALVES WITH CHERRIES	PANCAKES WITH MAPLE SYRUP, HONEY DEW MELON WITH COTTAGE CHEESE BAKED CUSTARD	HAMBURGER ON ROLL, POTATO SALAD, CUCUMBER SALAD CHOCOLATE PUDDING W/ TOPPING	NEW ENGLAND CLAM CHOWDER, SEALEG SALAD IN ROLL, COLESLAW RASPBERRY MOUSSE	CHICKEN NOODLE SOUP, TURKEY CLUB SANDWICH, CRANBERRY SAUCE DICED CANTALOUPE

SUNDAY	MONDAY	TUESDAY	WEDNESDAY	THURSDAY	FRIDAY	SATURDAY
ORANGE JUICE, HOT/COLD CEREAL CHOICE OF EGG TOAST/MUFFIN	WEEK JUNE 21 THRU JUNE 27 JULY 19 THRU JULY 25 AUGUST 16 THRU AUGUST 22 SEPT.13 THRU SEPT 19	DAILY ALTERNATES DINNER HAM, TURKEY, CHICKEN, MEATLOAF SUPPER CHOICE OF SOUP HAM, TURKEY, OR GRILL CHEESE SANDWICH		HB SNACK SUPPLEMENT ICE CREAM, CRACKERS, JUICE, SODA, MILK		
			LUNCH			
YANKEE POT ROAST W/GRAVY SCANDANAVIAN MIXED VEGETABLES, OVEN BROWN POTATO BANANA SPLIT	BAKED HAM W/RAISIN SAUCE, BAKED SWEET POTATO WHOLE GREEN BEANS PINEAPPLE UPSIDE DOWN CAKE	BEEF BURGANDY W/ EGG NOODLE, ORIENTAL VEGETABLES BOSTON CREAM PIE	CHICKEN CROQUETTE SHERRY SAUCE DUCHESS POTATO , PEAS&PIMENTOS ICE CREAM	SPAGHETTI WITH MEAT SAUCE ZUCCHINI SQUASH SMALL SALAD STRAWBERRY RHUBARB PIE	BAKED COD FISH TARTAR SAUCE BOULANGER POTATO , BROCCOLI NORMANDY W/ CHEESE SAUCE GRAPE NUT CUSTARD	STUFFED CABBAGE, WAXED BEANS, SMALL SALAD, DINNER ROLL, APPLE PIE
			DINNER			
VEGETABLE QUICHE, POTATO PANCAKES, SMALL SALAD, PEANUT BUTTER COOKIES	CHICKEN GUMBO SOUP, SMOKED SLICED TURKEY SANDWICH, FRUITED COTTAGE CHEESE PISTACHIO PUDDING	FRANKFURT ON ROLL, FRENCH FRIES, SLICED WATERMELON SPICE CAKE W/ VANILLA ICING	FRENCH TOAST, MAPLE SYRUP, BAKED SAUSAGE, PEACH GARNISH RICE PUDDING	COLD PLATE HAM SALAD, TUNA SALAD, COTTAGE CHEESE PICKLE BEETS LEMON MOUSSE	SPINACH & CHEESE OMLET, ITALIAN MIXED VEGETABLE ORANGE CRANBERRY MUFFIN MELON COMBO	CREAM OF CELERY SOUP CHICKEN SALAD ON WHOLE WHEAT CRANBERRY SAUCE CARROT CAKE W/ CREAM CHEESE ICING

FIGURE 4-8 Institutional Menu. *(Courtesy of Forest Farm Health Care Center, Middletown, RI.)*

SUNDAY	MONDAY	TUESDAY	WEDNESDAY	THURSDAY	FRIDAY	SATURDAY
ORANGE JUICE, HOT/COLD CEREAL CHOICE OF EGG, TOAST/ MUFFIN	WEEK JUNE 28 THRU JULY 4 JULY 26 THRU AUG. 1 AUG. 23 THRU AUG.29 SEPT. 20 THRU SEPT.26	DAILY ALTERNATES HAM, TURKEY, CHICKEN, MEATLOAF SUPPER CHOICE OF SOUP, HAM, TURKEY 1R GRILL CHEESE SANDWICH	BREAKFAST	HS SNACKES SUPPLEMENT ICE CREAM, CRACKERS JUICE, SODA, MILK		
			LUNCH			
ROAST PORK WITH GRAVY APPLE SAUCE MASHED POTATO WINTER MIXED VEGETABLE ICE CREAM	SHEPARDS PIE DUCHESS POTATO DICED CARROTS BLUEBERRY CHEESE CAKE	PAN FRIED SWEET& SOUR CHICKEN RICE PILAF JAPANESE MIXED VEGETABLE BANANA CREAM PIE	BAKED MEATLOAF MUSHROOM GRAVY MASHED POTATO SCANDANAVIAN MIXED VEGETABLE ICE CREAM	EGGPLANT PARMESAN ITALIAN MIXED VEGETABLE SMALL SALAD PEACH SHORT CAKE	BAKED POLLACK, ANNA POTATO, ZUCCHINI CASSEROLE LEMON MERINGUE PIE	FRANKS & BEANS SMALL SALAD, BROWN BREAD, WAXED BEANS RASPBERRY CAKE
			DINNER			
CHICKEN NOODLE SOUP GRILLED CHEESE PASTA SALAD BUTTERSOTCH PUDDING WITH TOPPING	HOT TURKEY SANDWICH W/GRAVY OVER TOAST FANCY MIXED VEGETABLE CRANBERRY SAUCE FRUIT COCKTAIL	BAKED MACARONI AND CHEESE SLICED BACON WHOLE GREEN BEANS M&M BROWNIE	PEA SOUP HAM SALAD ON CROISSANT APPLE RING GARNISH PEAR HALVES W/CHERRIES	SEAFOOD BISQUE TUNA MELT ON RYE PICKLE TAPIOCA PUDDING	CHICKEN NUGGETS POTATO PANCAKES PEAS AND PIMIENTOS CRANBERRY CRUNCH	CHICKEN GUMBO SOUP EGG SALAD ON WHEAT BREAD MELON VANILLA WHIP AND CHILL

SUNDAY	MONDAY	TUESDAY	WEDNESDAY	THURSDAY	FRIDAY	SATURDAY
ORANGE JUICE HOT/COLD CEREAL CHOICE OF EGG TOAST/ MUFFIN	WEEK JULY 5 THRU JULY11 AUG. 2 THRU AUG. 8 AUG. 30 THRU SEPT.5 SEPT.27 THRU OCT. 3	DAILY ALTERNATES HAM, TURKEY, CHICKEN, MEATLOAF, SUPPER CHOICE OF SOUP, HAM, TURKEY, OR GRILL CHEESE SANDWICH	BREAKFAST	HS SNACKS SUPPLEMENT ICE CREAM CRACKERS JUICE, SODA, MILK		
			LUNCH			
CORNED BEEF BOILED POTATO CABBAGE CARROTS ICE CREAM	BAKED HAM, BAKED POTATO, CUT GREEN BEANS, CREAM PIE	LASAGNA W/MEAT SAUCE ITALIAN MIX VEGETABLES, SMALL SALAD, GARLIC BREAD, CHOCOLATE CAKE	ROAST STUFF CHICKEN DUCHESS POTATO SCANDANAVIAN MIXED VEGETABLES ICE CREAM	SALISBURY STEAK MUSHROOM GRAVY BAKED POTATO WITH SOUR CREAM PEAS & PIMENTOS COCONUT CUSTARD PIE	BROILED SCALLOPS ANNA POTATO CHOPPED SPINACH WITH MUSHROOM STRAWBERRY MOUSSE	AMERICAN CHOP SUEY , MIXED VEGETABLES, SMALL SALAD, GINGER BREAD WITH TOPPING
			DINNER			
FRENCH TOAST W/FRESH STRAWBERRIES SLICED BACON FRUITED COTTAGE CHEESE ASSORTED COOKIES	MINESTRONE SOUP, ROAST BEEF SALAD SANDWICH CRABAPPLE GARNISH MARBLE PUDDING W/TOPPING	BEEF NOODLE SOUP, GRILLED CHEESE SANDWICH, PASTA SALAD GARNISH PEACHES N CREAM	CREAM OF TOMATO SOUP, TUNA SALAD ON CROISSANT PICKLE GARNISH CHERRY BAVARIAN PIE	CHICKEN PATTIE IN ROLL, FRENCH FRIES, THREE BEAN SALAD SLICED WATERMELON	CHEESE OMELET, HOT BLUEBERRY MUFFIN, SCANDANAVIAN MIX VEGETABLES HEAVENLY HASH	CHICKEN RICE SOUP, SEALEG SALAD IN BUN LETTUCE & TOMATO LEMON PUDDING

FIGURE 4-8 Continued.

Room Service Menus

Type of Menu. The room service menu can be à la carte, semi à la carte, or prix fixe. The menu can consist of a complete wine and liquor list, appetizer selections, soups, salads, hot and cold entrées, hot and cold sandwiches, vegetables, potatoes, pasta, rice, and an assortment of desserts. It is important that room service items have good hot and cold holding qualities, for example, stuffed filet of sole and a tossed salad.

Food Availability. All food items on the room service menu are usually included on the main dining room menu; therefore, there is no difficulty in obtaining food items.

Equipment. The most important piece of equipment that all foodservice operations should have is a server table.

Expense Level. Room service menu items are usually expensive due to the added service of delivering food to the rooms. Therefore, a room service menu item is often more expensive than the actual item on the dining room menu.

Atmosphere. Room service menus often will look like miniature versions of the main dining room menu, fitting in with the decor and theme of the hotel.

Proficiency. Many room service menus have very elaborate items that require special skills on the part of the kitchen staff. In no other menu do skills play such an important role with regard to service personnel. The waitstaff are completely on their own from the time that they leave the kitchen until they arrive at the guest's room.

Customer Makeup. Room service customers expect excellent food because of the high price of the menu items.

Type of Service. Orders are phoned in by guests and are placed on serving trays or tables and then delivered to the guest's room.

Type of Menu. The style of menu (Figure 4-9) is à la carte, semi à la carte, and prix fixe. The juice, cereals, fruits, breakfast specialties, and side orders are à la carte. The eggs and omelets are served with a choice of Southern Grits or Country Style potatoes, and toast or biscuits. The complete breakfast offers juice, eggs, pancakes, bacon, homemade bak-

Room Service
Breakfast Menu
6:00am – 11:30am

First Choices
Freshly Squeezed Orange, Grapefruit, or Carrot Juice
V8, Cranberry, Tomato, or Apple Juice
4.50

Seasonal Fresh Fruit
6.50

Mixed Berries with Whipped Cream and Lemon Curd, Oatmeal Tuile
8.00

Chilled Indian River Grapefruit
With Basil Honey Syrup
8.00

Red and Yellow Watermelon
Marinated With Mint
6.50

Swiss Bircher Muesli, Apples, Dried Cherries, and Almonds
8.00

Old-Fashioned Oatmeal, Milk, Brown Sugar and Raisins
6.50

"Stone Ground" Grits, Sharp Cheddar Cheese
6.50

Homemade Granola with Honey Yogurt
and Stewed Peaches
7.00

Warm Croissant, Shaved Ham, Scrambled Eggs, Cheddar Cheese
13.50

Cholesterol Free Egg White Omelet with Roasted Vegetables
12.50

Grilled Bagel with Scrambled Eggs and Smoked Salmon
15.00

Side Orders
Basket of Homemade Breakfast Bakeries
8.00

Smoked Bacon, Country Sausage, Cured Ham
4.00

Hashed Brown Potatoes
2.50

English Muffin or Toasted Breads
2.50

Bagel and Cream Cheese
5.50

Complete Breakfasts

THE AMERICAN
Choice of Juice
Two Eggs Prepared any Style
Silver Dollar Pancakes
Applewood Smoked Bacon
Breakfast Bakeries or Toast
Coffee, Decaffeinated Coffee or Hot Tea
19.00

THE LENOX
Choice of Juice
Mixed Berries with Whipped Cream and Lemon Curd
Classical Poached Eggs Benedict
Steamed Asparagus, Hollandaise Sauce
Breakfast Bakeries or Toast
Coffee, Decaffeinated Coffee or Hot Tea
21.00

Breakfast Specialties
Smoked Salmon, Sliced Red Onion, Tomato, Fresh Bagel and Cream Cheese
15.00

Pecan Raisin and Apple Bread "French Toast", Vanilla Sauce
11.00

Crisp Lemon Poppyseed Waffle, Blueberry Compote
12.00

Buttermilk Griddle Cakes, Bananas or Wild Berries, Southern Praline Pecan Syrup
11.00

Berries, Melons and Tropical Fruits
With Banana Nut Bread and Basil Honey Yogurt
12.00

Eggs and Omelets
(Served with your choice of Southern Grits or Country Style Potatoes
and Toast or Biscuits)

Two Farm Eggs, any style
9.50
Egg Beaters
7.50
with Smoked Bacon, Cured Ham or Country Sausage
13.00
with New York Steak
18.00

Three-Egg Omelet Prepared to Order:
Choice of Ham, Peppers, Tomatoes, Mushrooms, Shrimp, Goat Cheese, Cheddar or
Herbs
13.50

Open-Faced Country Omelet with Potatoes, Spinach, Portuguese Sausage
and Goat Cheese
14.50

Poached Eggs on Corned Beef and Mushroom Hash,
Grain Mustard Hollandaise
14.00

Classical Eggs Benedict, Hollandaise Sauce, Steamed Asparagus
14.50

THE CONTINENTAL
Choice of Juice
Basket of Homemade Bakeries or Toast
Coffee, Decaffeinated Coffee or Hot Tea
16.00

THE FITNESS
Choice of Fruit Juice or Carrot Juice
Seasonal Fresh Fruit
Dry Cereal with Skim Milk
Coffee, Decaffeinated Coffee, or Hot Tea
15.50

Beverages
Freshly Brewed Regular or Decaffeinated Coffee
Small (Three Cups)
3.50
Large (Six Cups)
6.00
Whole or Skim Milk
3.00
Pot of Hot Chocolate
4.50
Tea Assortment
Darjeeling, Earl Grey, English Breakfast, Chamomile, Decaffeinated, Mint or Japanese
Green
3.50

FIGURE 4-9 Room Service Menu. *(Courtesy Ritz Carlton Buckhead, Atlanta, GA.)*

All Day Dining
11:30am – 10:30pm

Appetizers and Soups

Georgia Farm Lettuces, Honey Lemon and Thyme Vinaigrette - * Cuisine Vitale
7.00

Classic Caesar Salad, Garlic Croutons, Shaved Parmigiano
8.50

Chilled Gulf Shrimp Cocktail with Tomato Horseradish Sauce
12.00

On The Vine Ripened Tomatoes, Vidalia Onions
Mozzarella and Herb Caper Vinaigrette - * Cuisine Vitale
10.00

House Smoked Salmon, Traditional Garniture, Toast Points
12.00

The Café's Signature Jumbo Lump Crab Cakes
11.00

Homemade Foie Gras Terrine
Toasted Brioche, Fruit Chutney
9.50

The Ritz-Carlton, Boston's Original Clam Chowder
8.00

Pisto Soup
10.00

Today's Soup Selection
7.00

Selection of American Farm Cheeses
With Dried Fruits and Nuts
12.00

Imported Caspian Caviar, Served with Blinis and Classical Garnish
Beluga
85.00/oz.

Ossettra
65.00/oz.

Main Course Salads

Classic Caesar Salad with Grilled Chicken Breast
15.00
Or Grilled Jumbo Prawns
19.00

Seared Ahi Tuna "Nicoise" Salad, Olive Croutons
Tarragon Vinaigrette - * Cuisine Vitale
17.00

Southern Fried Catfish Salad

Smoked Chicken Cobb Salad
13.00

Sandwiches

Smoked Turkey "Club" on Multi Grain Bread, French Fries
12.00

Grilled 8 oz. Sirloin Hamburger, Choice of Cheese, French Fries
9.50

Portobello Mushroom, Goat Cheese, Roasted Peppers and Arugula on Focaccia Bread
11.00

Entrées

Certified Black Angus 14 oz. New York Steak, Béarnaise Sauce, Baked Potato
Jumbo Asparagus
26.00

Grilled Salmon Fillet, Braised Fennel and Basmati Rice - * Cuisine Vitale
21.00

Roasted Half Chicken, Natural Jus, Whipped Potatoes
19.50

Spinach Tagliatelli, Smoked Salmon, Tomato, Asparagus
18.00

Farfalle "A la Norma", Capers, Nicoise Olives,
Garlic Oil - * Cuisine Vitale
16.00

Today's Vegetarian Creation - * Cuisine Vitale
20.00

Late Night Menu
10:30pm – 6:00am

Appetizers

Chilled Jumbo Gulf Shrimp Cocktail, Tomato Horseradish Sauce
12.00

Classic Caesar Salad, Garlic Croutons, Shaved Parmigiano
8.50
With Chicken
15.00
With Jumbo Prawns
19.00

House Smoked Salmon, Traditional Garniture
Toast Points
12.00

Entrees

Sirloin Hamburger, Choice of Cheese, French Fries
9.50

Grilled Chicken "Club", Multi Grain Bread, French Fries
12.00

Portobello Mushrooms, Goat Cheese, Roasted Peppers and Arugula on Focaccia Bread
11.00
With Chicken 14.00

Three-Egg Omelet with French Fries
13.50

Grilled Prime New York Steak, Bordelaise Sauce, Baked Potato
28.00

Grilled Salmon Fillet, Jasmine Rice, Hollandaise Sauce
21.00

Rigatoni with Stewed Tomatoes, Capers, Nicoise Olives and Garlic Oil – *Cuisine Vitale*
16.00

FIGURE 4-9 Continued.

Homemade Pizzas
(Our Pizzas are 12 inches, 6 slices)

Four Cheese Pizza
Gorgonzola, Parmigiano, Goat Cheese and Mozzarella
15.00

Prosciutto Pizza
Prosciutto, Fine Herbs, Wild Mushrooms, Asparagus and Mozzarella
14.00

Chicken Pizza
Grilled Chicken, Caramelized Onions, Goat Cheese, Sun-Dried Tomatoes, Cilantro
15.00

Vegetarian Pizza
Pesto Crusted with Grilled Vegetables
13.50

Children's Selections
Chicken Noodle Soup
2.50
Peanut Butter & Jelly Sandwich
5.00
Grilled Cheese Sandwich, French Fries
6.00
Breaded Chicken Tenders, French Fries
7.00
Double Fudge Brownies with Ice Cream

Desserts
Traditional Crème Brulee, Fresh Berries

Southern Pecan Pie, Caramel Rum Sauce

Lemon Cheese Cake, Blackberry Marmalade

The Ultimate Chocolate Cake
Served with Coffee Ice Cream and Mocha Emulsion

Upside Down Caramelized Apple Tart
Cinnamon Whipped Cream

7.00

Selection of Homemade Sorbets and Ice Creams

Homemade Pizzas
(Our Pizza is 12 inches, 6 Slices)

Four Cheese Pizza
Gorgonzola, Parmigiano, Goat Cheese and Mozzarella
15.00

Prosciutto Pizza
Prosciutto, Fine Herbs, Wild Mushrooms, Asparagus and Mozzarella
14.00

Chicken Pizza
Grilled Chicken, Caramelized Onions, Goat Cheese, Sun-Dried Tomatoes, Cilantro
15.00

Vegetarian Pizza
Pesto Crusted with Grilled Vegetables
13.50

Desserts

Fresh Sliced Seasonal Fruit Plate, Banana Nut Bread
12.00

Homemade Ice Creams or Fruit Sorbets
7.00

Traditional Crème Brûlée, Fresh Berries
7.00

Southern Pecan Pie, Caramel Rum Sauce
7.00

FIGURE 4-9 Continued.

eries or toast, and a beverage for an all-inclusive price. Appetizers, soups, salads, sandwiches, entrées, pizzas, and desserts are offered à la carte.

Food Availability. Many of the food items on the room service menu are included on the main dining room menu; therefore, there should be no difficulty in purchasing these food items.

Equipment. The room service menu requires a server table and the same equipment that is used in the dining room to serve food.

Expense Level. The expense level is moderate to high. Juices cost $4.50; French Toast, $11; Smoked Chicken Cobb Salad, $13; and the Certified Black Angus 14 oz. New York Steak, Béarnaise Sauce, Baked Potato, Jumbo Asparagus combination, $26. Traditional Crème Brulée, Fresh Berries is priced at $7.

Atmosphere. The Ritz Carlton Buckhead's extensive room service menu reflects the hotel's ability to accommodate and to please a sophisticated clientele with a variety of tastes.

Proficiency. The chefs must have a good culinary background in order to prepare the array of appetizers, soups, salads, entrées, and desserts that are presented on the menu.

Customer Makeup. The customers are business people, families, and domestic and international tourists.

Type of Service. Room service orders are placed by phone. The orders are placed on server tables and delivered to the rooms.

Ethnic Menus

Type of Menu. An ethnic menu can be either semi à la carte or à la carte. In most cases, an ethnic menu offers cuisine that is representative of a particular geographical area or a specific country. The descriptions of the appetizers, soups, salads, entrées, vegetables, potatoes, and desserts are often written in the language used in the country from which the cuisine is derived. An accompanying English translation should also appear for those who wish to experience the cuisine but who do not have a grasp of the language.

Food Availability. Acquiring certain food supplies can be problematic for items on ethnic menus. Before producing or printing the menu, the planner of an ethnic menu should carefully research the availability, costs, and delivery time of supplies.

Equipment. Assuring that you have the right equipment to handle the items is especially important when you are planning an ethnic menu. Chinese restaurants have woks, and Italian restaurants usually need pasta makers.

Expense Level. The cost of the meal can range from low to high, depending on the restaurant's concept.

Atmosphere. Decor is extremely important in an ethnic restaurant. For example, brightly colored tiles, waitstaff dressed in traditional costumes, and Mariachi music playing in the background are expected by diners in a Mexican restaurant.

Proficiency. The cooks and the service personnel must be highly skilled in ethnic cuisine. To make food as authentic as possible, cooks or chefs with training in such cuisine should be employed. Service personnel who are able to communicate both in the native language and in English are a definite asset.

Customer Makeup. The clientele is made up of both local and out-of-town customers.

Type of Service. Service in most ethnic restaurants is American. French restaurants might offer French service, and higher-end restaurants in this category might even offer Russian service.

Type of Menu. Daniel offers a prix fixe menu (Figure 4-10), which includes an appetizer, salad, and entrée.

Food Availability. Ingredients needed for the preparation of the offerings listed are obtained through local purveyors in order to guarantee freshness of product.

Equipment. The Chilled Young Carrot Soup with Lobster, Lime and Coriander; and the Tournedos of Striped Bass with Porcini, Marrow Toast, Sautéed Potatoes and Onions with Purslane and a Bordelaise Sauce require a flat-top range or an open burner. The Roasted Veal Medallion and Braised Shank with a Swiss Chard Galette, Toasted Almonds, Lemon, Olives and Spanish Capers require an oven as well as a flat-top range or open burner.

Expense Level. The cost, at $72 per person, is high for a three-course meal.

Atmosphere. The simple Daniel logo on the front cover of the menu exudes the richness and elegance for which the Mayfair Hotel is known. The menu listings are first presented in French to represent the ethnic cuisine offered by the restaurant and are followed by a translation in English to better accommodate guests.

Proficiency. The front- and back-of-the-house employees must be skilled. The waitstaff must be able to pronounce the menu items correctly and also must have a thorough knowledge of how the food items are prepared. The chefs have to know a variety of cooking techniques, such as braising, roasting, sautéing, and smoking.

FIGURE 4-10 Ethnic Menu. *(Courtesy of Daniel, New York, NY.)*

DANIEL

LE VELOUTE DE MELON DE CAVAILLON
CREVETTES ET CITRONNELLE
Chilled French Melon Velouté with Gulf Shrimp
Flavored with Lemongrass, Purple Basil and Kafir Leaves

LE POTAGE DE CAROTTES NOUVELLES, HOMARD ET CITRON VERT
Chilled Young Carrot Soup with Lobster, Lime and Coriander

LE THON CRU ET RIS DE VEAU CROUSTILLANT "VITELLO TONNATO"
Marinated Raw Tuna and Crispy Sweetbreads with Tonnato Sauce
Celery Leaves, Purslane and Hazelnuts

LES LEGUMES D'ETE ET HOMARD AU CURRY, MANGUE ET BASILIC
Salad of Lobster and Summer Vegetables
Mango, Basil and a Light Curry Dressing

LA BALLOTTINE DE FOIE GRAS ET FIGUES VIOLETTES CONFITES AU PORTO
Duck Foie Gras Terrine with Spiced Mission Figs and a Port Wine Reduction $10

LA TERRINE DE QUEUE DE BŒUF ET FOIE GRAS A LA TRUFFE NOIRE
Oxtail and Foie Gras Terrine, Black Truffle Dressing and Artichokes $10

LE CAVIAR ET SAUMON FUME DE DANIEL BOULUD

| Beluga 1 ¼ oz | Golden Oscetra 1 ½ oz | Smoked Salmon |
| à la carte $115 / sup. $90 | à la carte $85 / sup. $65 | |

A CELEBRATION OF SUMMER TOMATOES

LA SOUPE GLACEE DE TOMATES ET LEGUMES
COMPOTE D'AUBERGINE ET PISTOU
Chilled Tomato Soup with Lavender Eggplant Compote and Arugula Pesto

LA SALADE DE CRABE DU MAINE A LA GELEE DE TOMATE ET FENOUIL
Maine Peeky Toe Crab Salad in a Light Tomato Gelée with Fennel and Avocado

LES RAVIOLES DE NEUF HERBES AUX CHANTERELLES
COULIS DE TOMATE ET FLEUR DE COURGETTE
Ravioli of Nine Herbs with Chanterelles
Tomato Coulis and Crisp Zucchini Flowers

FIGURE 4-10 Continued.

DANIEL

LA LOTTE ET HOMARD ROULEES AU LARD
COULIS DE MAIS ET FONDUE DE RACINES TRUFFEES
Monkfish and Lobster Wrapped in Spice-Cured Country Bacon
Sweet Corn Coulis and Truffled Young Root Vegetables

LE TOURNEDOS DE BAR POELE AUX CEPES
CROUTONS DE MOELLE, POMMES LYONNAISES ET POURPIER
Tournedos of Striped Bass with Porcini, Marrow Toast
Sautéed Potatoes and Onions with Purslane and a Bordelaise Sauce

LE SAUMON ROTI EN CROUTE DE FEVES, GIROLLES ET SARRIETTE
Roasted Alaskan King Salmon with a Crust of Fava Beans and Chanterelles
Sweet Onion Compote with a Tarragon Béarnaise and Savory Jus

L'ESPADON ROTI A LA PLANCHA AUX PIMENTS D'ESPELETTE ET JAMBON DE VIRGINIE
Hot Steel-Seared Swordfish with Basque Pimentos
Cured Virginia Ham, Stewed Peppers and Burnette Greens

LA PAUPIETTE DE SEA BASS CROUSTILLANTE AU VIN ROUGE
Paupiette of Black Sea Bass Wrapped in a Crisp Potato Shell
Tender Leeks and a Syrah Sauce

LE POULET ROTI A LA BROCHE FOURRE D'HERBES
CASSEROLE D'HARICOTS GRATINES ET TOMATES
Spit-Roasted Chicken Rubbed with Herbs, Garlic and Peppercorns
Fricassée of Summer Beans and Tomato

LE MEDAILLON DE BŒUF PIQUE A LA TRUFFE
BOULANGERE DE POMMES NOUVELLES AUX CEPES
Roasted Beef Medallion Wrapped with Pancetta and Black Truffle
Braised Potato and Porcini Gratin with Haricots Verts

LE PIGEON GLACE AUX EPICES ET CHUTNEY DE GROSEILLES
Glazed Spiced Squab with a Red Currant Chutney, Sautéed Young Spinach and Kohlrabi

LE CARRE D'AGNEAU EN CROUTE DE PIGNONS ET CITRON, JUS A LA TAPENADE
Rack of Lamb with a Lemon-Pine Nut Crust and Chickpea Fries
Stuffed Piquillo Pepper, Eggplant Caviar and a Tapenade Jus

LE MIGNON ET JARRET DE VEAU AUX SAVEURS DE LA MEDITERRANNEE
Roasted Veal Medallion and Braised Shank with a Swiss Chard Galette
Toasted Almonds, Lemon, Olives and Spanish Capers

Three Course Prix Fixe
$72

FIGURE 4-10 Continued.

Customer Makeup. The clientele is comprised of business people, travel guests, and couples who are celebrating special occasions.

Type of Service. The service is French.

Specialty Menus

Type of Menu. The specialty menu is usually semi à la carte. Specialty houses offer steak, seafood, or chicken, for the most part. At a seafood specialty restaurant, it is common for seafood selections to appear in the appetizer, soup, salad, and entrée sections of the menu. A number of cooking techniques—baking, broiling, frying, grilling, poaching, sautéing, smoking, and steaming—are used in the preparation of such items.

In planning a menu for a specialty restaurant, it is important to remember to offer other items as well. For example, a seafood restaurant might offer a chicken item in order to accommodate those who do not like seafood or who are allergic to it and those who are accompanying guests who enjoy the house's specialties.

Food Availability. The most important factor in serving seafood is freshness. Seafood should be purchased on a daily basis, preferably from local fisheries, if location permits. Steaks should be USDA Prime or USDA Choice.

Equipment. The size and complexity of the menu make it necessary to have a fully equipped kitchen, especially if you are specializing in seafood. Less sophisticated equipment is required when the specialty is steak or chicken.

Expense Level. The price of the menu items depends on the concept selected. Seafood and steaks are usually moderately to expensively priced.

Atmosphere. Seafood restaurants often use a nautical motif and decor. Lobster traps, fish netting, and anchors create a seafaring atmosphere. Steak restaurants often will display ranch motifs.

Proficiency. In most specialty houses, the wide range of dishes and preparation methods require that professional cooks be hired. Service personnel should be trained in American or modified Russian service. Modified Russian service is sometimes used in seafood houses. Wait-staff also should have a knowledge of the preparation of dishes.

Customer Makeup. The clientele consists of tourists, business people, couples, and families.

Type of Service. Service in a specialty house is usually American. However, in many seafood houses, a number of dishes are served in casseroles, which will usually require modified Russian service. Modified Russian service requires that the waitstaff use a serving spoon and a fork to serve a portion of the casserole onto a dinner plate.

Type of Menu. The style of menu (Figure 4-11) is à la carte and semi à la carte. The à la carte items consist of appetizer, soup, salad, sandwich, side dishes, and dessert items. Semi à la carte choices include a salad or a cup of soup, and one side dish with the entrée.

The Hereford House specializes in beef. Beef is offered in the soups, salads, and entrées.

Food Availability. All items on the menu can be purchased from local purveyors.

Equipment. The equipment needed to produce this menu is as follows: soups require a flat-top range or an open burner; Prime Rib and Cedar Planked Salmon requires the use of an oven; the BBQ Pork Ribs require a smoker; and the Kansas City Strip, Filet Mignon, and Steak Kabob require a broiler.

Expense Level. The Hereford House's menu is moderately to high priced, with costs ranging from $2.75 for a cup of Steak Soup to $36.95 for the Filet & Lobster.

Atmosphere. The menu style and offerings reflect the theme and specialty of the house.

Proficiency. Cooks need to be skilled in broiling technique, and the waitstaff should be knowledgeable about the preparation of the menu items.

Customer Makeup. The customer makeup is predominately families, tourists, and local business people.

Type of Service. The service is American.

Wine and Dessert Menus

Wine and dessert menus can be incorporated into the dinner menu or can be separate menus dedicated solely to wines or desserts. An extensive selection of wines or desserts usually will require a special wine or

★★★★ KANSAS CITY'S ORIGINAL ★★★★

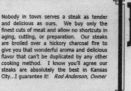

HEREFORD HOUSE

EST. 1957

Nobody in town serves a steak as tender and delicious as ours. We buy only the finest cuts of meat and allow no shortcuts in aging, cutting, or preparation. Our steaks are broiled over a hickory charcoal fire to give you that wonderful aroma and delicious flavor that can't be duplicated by any other cooking method. I know you'll agree our steaks are absolutely the best in Kansas City...I guarantee it! *Rod Anderson, Owner*

Planning a meeting, party, or banquet? The Hereford House offers the finest private dining facilities. Ask to see our menus.

Share "The Best Steaks in Kansas City" with your family, friends, or clients. You can send the same corn-fed beef, like we serve at the Hereford House, anywhere in the continental United States. For more info call 816-842-6718, or order steaks online: www.herefordhouse.com

APPETIZERS

STUFFED MUSHROOMS
WITH CRAB AND SHRIMP IN A CREAMY CHEESE FILLING.
$6.95

"BUFFALO" WINGS
ONE POUND OF FRIED CHICKEN DRUMMIES WITH MILD BUFFALO & RANCH DIPPING SAUCES.
$6.95

SANTA FE GOAT CHEESE
WITH SUN-DRIED TOMATO PESTO AND CRUSHED ALMONDS, AND CRISP GARLIC TOAST.
$5.95

SHRIMP COCKTAIL
WITH HORSERADISH COCKTAIL SAUCE.
$9.95

ESCARGOT
BAKED IN MUSHROOM CAPS WITH GARLIC HERB BUTTER.
$7.95

ONION RINGS
FRIED GOLDEN BROWN AND DUSTED WITH SPECIAL SEASONINGS.
$5.50

GRILLED SHRIMP
WITH TEQUILA-LIME BBQ SAUCE.
$10.95

HH CARPACCIO
CHARRED RARE PRIME SIRLOIN, SLICED THIN & SERVED CHILLED WITH CHIPOTLE MAYONNAISE.
$6.95

STEAK SOUP
A KANSAS CITY TRADITION!
CUP $3.25   BOWL $4.25

CHEF'S SPECIAL SOUP
PREPARED FRESH DAILY.
CUP $2.75   BOWL $3.75

SALADS

CAESAR SALAD
$6.25

CROWN YOUR CAESAR:
GRILLED CHICKEN BREAST...$4.00
GRILLED TENDERLOIN KABOB...$7.00
GRILLED SALMON FILLET...$6.00

GRILLED VEGETABLE SALAD
WITH BALSAMIC VINAIGRETTE.
$9.95

YOUR SALAD DRESSING CHOICES INCLUDE: OUR *SIGNATURE* HEREFORD HOUSE CHEDDAR CHEESE *OR* CREAMY ITALIAN, RANCH, BLUE CHEESE, 1000 ISLAND, HONEY MUSTARD, FRENCH, BALSAMIC VINAIGRETTE, AND FAT-FREE ITALIAN *OR* RANCH.

STEAKS

INCLUDES CHOICE OF SALAD OR CUP OF SOUP, AND ONE SIDE DISH.

KANSAS CITY STRIP
THE STEAK THAT MADE KC FAMOUS!
12 OZ, $21.95
16 OZ, $26.95
24 OZ, $32.95

FILET MIGNON
GUARANTEED CENTER CUT.
6 OZ, $22.50
9 OZ, $27.50
12 OZ, $32.50

T-BONE
22 OZ, $29.95

RIBEYE STEAK
16 OZ, $20.95
20 OZ, $23.95
COWBOY CUT, $29.95

PRIME TOP SIRLOIN
AN ESPECIALLY FLAVORFUL CUT.
12 OZ, $20.95
BASEBALL CUT, $23.95

FILET & LOBSTER
OUR FILET AND 9 OZ LOBSTER TAIL, WITH DRAWN BUTTER & LEMON.
6 OZ FILET, $36.95
9 OZ FILET, $41.95

FILET & GRILLED SHRIMP
OUR FILET AND FOUR SHRIMP.
6 OZ FILET, $28.95
9 OZ FILET, $33.95

PRIME RIB
THE CHOICEST CUT OF FINE HEREFORD HOUSE BEEF OVEN ROASTED WITH SPECIAL SEASONINGS.
12 OZ, $20.95
18 OZ, $24.95
24 OZ, $28.95

LARGER STEAKS AVAILABLE UPON REQUEST!

FOR YOUR STEAK

DRESS YOUR STEAK WITH ONE OF OUR SIGNATURE ACCOMPANIMENTS.

BÉARNAISE SAUCE
WHISKEY SAUCE
CRACKED PEPPER & BLUE CHEESE
BORDELAISE SAUCE
DIJON & BROWN SUGAR GLAZED
$1.50
PORTOBELLO MUSHROOMS
$3.95

TEMPERATURE GUIDE

RARE: COOL RED CENTER.
MEDIUM RARE: WARM RED CENTER.
MEDIUM: HOT PINK CENTER.
MEDIUM WELL: SLIGHT PINK CENTER.
WELL DONE: COOKED THROUGHOUT.

CHUCKWAGON SPECIALTIES

INCLUDES CHOICE OF SALAD OR CUP OF SOUP, AND ONE SIDE DISH.

STEAK KABOB
PRIME SIRLOIN MARINATED IN OUR SPECIAL SAUCE & GRILLED.
$15.95

GROUND SIRLOIN
FLAVORED WITH PEPPERS & ONIONS.
$13.95

CHICKEN BREAST
SEMI-BONELESS, MARINATED AND PAN ROASTED.
$14.95

BEEF SHORT RIBS
SLOW COOKED UNTIL TENDER IN A HEARTY BORDELAISE SAUCE.
$17.95

BBQ PORK RIBS
A FULL SLAB OF TENDER BABY-BACK PORK RIBS, GLAZED WITH BBQ SAUCE & SERVED WITH COWBOY BEANS.
$17.95

SEAFOOD

INCLUDES CHOICE OF SALAD OR CUP OF SOUP, AND A SIDE DISH.

FRESH CATCH OF THE DAY
ASK YOUR SERVER ABOUT TODAY'S SPECIAL SELECTION.
MARKET PRICE

LOBSTER TAIL
WITH DRAWN BUTTER & LEMON.
$26.95

CEDAR PLANKED SALMON
OVEN ROASTED ON A CEDAR PLANK FOR A SPECIAL FLAVOR, WITH GARLIC HERB BUTTER AND VEGETABLES.
$19.95

SIDE DISHES

BAKED POTATO
TWICE BAKED POTATO
GARLIC MASHED POTATOES
FRENCH FRIES
ONION RINGS
WILD RICE PILAF
SAUTÉED GARLIC SPINACH
VEGETABLE OF THE DAY
BAKED COWBOY BEANS
$2.95

DESSERTS

PREPARED FRESH DAILY BY OUR TALENTED PASTRY CHEFS. YOUR SERVER WILL SHOW YOU TODAY'S SPECIAL SELECTIONS!

SMOKING PERMITTED IN THE BAR ONLY.
18% GRATUITY ADDED ON PARTIES OF 8 OR MORE.
HH2F JULY '00

David Reed, General Manager

Erik Hyre, Executive Chef

FIGURE 4-11 Specialty Menu. *(Courtesy of Hereford House Restaurant, Kansas City, MO.)*

WINDOWS

Wine List

We have organized our wine list to help you select the taste and style of wine that you enjoy most from beginning to end and within each sub-heading, the wines are listed from those that are lighter and fruitier in style to those that are heavier and fuller in body. This means that wines with taste similarities are grouped together. We hope that this encourages you to experiment a bit and try some new and different wines. If we can assist you in your wine and food experience, please ask.

		Glass	Bottle
Sparkling Wines Slightly Sweet To Drier And Fuller Bodied			
101.	Hyatt Private Cuvee, California		22.00
102.	Domaine Chandon, Hyatt Cuvee		33.00
103.	Freixenet, Cordon Negro (Split), Spain		8.00
104.	Perrier Jouet, France		65.00
105.	Nicholas Feuillate Cuvee Palmes d'Or, France		145.00
Light, Fruity, Blush and White Wines Lightly Sweet To Just Off-Dry			
111.	Glen Ellen, White Zinfandel, California	5.25	24.00
112.	Beringer White Zinfandel, California		26.00
113.	Forest Fire White Merlot by Forest Glen, California		26.00
114.	Sterling Sauvignon Blanc, North Coast California	6.50	34.00
115.	Ecco Domani Pinot Grigio, Italy	6.25	31.00
116.	Santa Margherita Pinot Grigio, Italy		46.00
Medium Oaked To Fuller Bodied White Wine			
120.	Arianna Chardonnay, California	5.25	24.00
122.	Rivercrest Chardonnay, California		25.00
123.	Caliterra Chardonnay, Chile		29.00
124.	Talus Chardonnay, California	5.50	29.00
125.	Callaway Chardonnay, California	5.75	30.00
126.	Chateau St. Michelle Chardonnay, Washington	6.50	34.00
127.	Kendall-Jackson Chardonnay, Sonoma County	7.00	37.00
128.	Clos Du Bois Chardonnay, California		35.00
129.	Robert Mondavi Chardonnay, California		40.00
130.	Merryvale Chardonnay, Napa Valley		52.00
Light And Fruity To Medium Bodied Red Wines			
131.	Ravenswood "Vintners Blend" Zinfandel, California		36.00
132.	Rivercrest Merlot, California	5.00	25.00
133.	Caliterra Merlot, Chile		29.00
134.	Glass Mountain Merlot, California		34.00
135.	Robert Mondavi Coastal Merlot, California		37.00
136.	Farallon Merlot, Coastal California	6.50	34.00
137.	Talus Pinot Noir, California	5.50	26.00
138.	Morgan Pinot Noir, California		54.00
Moderately Tannic, To Fuller Bodied Red Wines			
140.	Arianna Cabernet Sauvignon, California	5.00	25.00
141.	Rivercrest Cabernet Sauvignon, California	5.00	25.00
142.	Talus Cabernet Sauvignon, California	5.50	29.00
143.	Glass Mountain Cabernet Sauvignon, California		34.00
144.	Buena Vista Cabernet Sauvignon, California		31.00
145.	Kendall-Jackson Cabernet Sauvignon, Sonoma County	7.50	41.00
146.	Wolf Blass Cabernet Sauvignon, Australia	6.75	35.00
147.	Hardys Cabernet/Shiraz Blend, Australia		33.00
148.	Merryvale Cabernet Sauvignon, Napa Valley		54.00
149.	Robert Mondavi Cabernet Sauvignon, Napa Valley		66.00

8/00

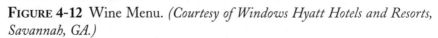

FIGURE 4-12 Wine Menu. *(Courtesy of Windows Hyatt Hotels and Resorts, Savannah, GA.)*

dessert menu. Wine and dessert menus should complement the menu offerings and should reflect the degree of sophistication of the restaurant.

A wine list is usually prepared by a cellar master. It includes a variety of types and selections of wines, which range in price. The name of the wine and its origin, the year of vintage, the price, and the bin number usually are included on a more extensive wine menu. A description of the style, taste, flavor, and pairing compatibility with certain foods also may be offered.

Dessert Menus may be used to list and describe house offerings. They may be employed in and of themselves or in conjunction with a dessert tray or a dessert cart presentation, listing products with limited holding qualities, such as Baked Alaska or sorbet. Some dessert menus also list specialty coffees, teas, and after-dinner drinks.

Menu Listing	Wine Recommendations
Appetizers	Dry white, sherry, or Champagne
Entrée of:	
Beef	Vigorous, robust, full-bodied, hearty or spicy red
Chicken	Crisp, full-bodied white, or silky, soft red
Duck	Crisp, full-bodied white, or silky, soft red
Fish	Dry white, medium dry white
Ham	Rosé, dry white, medium dry white
Lamb	Vigorous, robust, full-bodied, hearty or spicy red
Pheasant	Vigorous, robust, full-bodied, hearty or spicy red
Pork	Rosé, dry white, medium dry white
Seafood	Dry white, medium dry white
Turkey	Crisp, full-bodied white, or silky, soft red, or Champagne
Veal	Crisp, full-bodied white, or silky, soft red
Venison	Vigorous, robust, full-bodied, hearty or spicy red
Desserts	Sweet wine or semisweet sparkling wine

FIGURE 4-13 Food and Wine Pairing Chart.

DESSERTS

Plum creme fraiche tartlette with cornmeal crust
and ginger ice cream

Chocolate ice cream sandwich with coconut pecan
macaroons and coconut caramel sauce

Summer berry pudding with whipped cream

Apricot sorbet and blackberry sherbert
with vanilla bean shortbread

Fromage blanc cheese cake with
zinfandel poached figs

*Bittersweet chocolate mousse with filo
crisps and raspberry sauce

* Vegan Dessert

DESSERT WINES

1900 *Nieport LBV Port 1994*	4 oz glass:	4.50
1905 *York Creek Port*	2.5 oz glass:	6.25
1907 *Fonseca 20 year old Tawny*	2.5 oz glass:	8.00
1908 *Quinta do Noval Port 1995*	2.5 oz glass:	7.00
1910 *Warre's Port 1977*	2.5 oz glass:	18.00
1912 *Blandys 10 year Malmsey*	2.5 oz glass:	6.00
1916 *Muscat Beaumes de Venise 1994*	4 oz glass:	4.50
1920 *Ch. Roumieu Lacoste Sauterne 97*	2.5 oz glass:	5.75
1925 *Ch. Climens Sauternes - Barsac 1996*	½ bot:	50.00
1929 **Chateau d'Yquem* Sauternes 1989*	½ bot:	150.00
1938 **Tokay Pinot Gris Rotenberg "Wintzenheim"*		
S.G.N. (Zind Humbrecht) 1991	½ bot:	100.00
1942 **Gewurztraminer "Rangen" Clos St Urbain Grand Cru*		
S.G.N. (Zind Humbrecht) 1993	5th:	240.00

**Cellar Temperature*

Espresso Drinks

Espresso	2.25	Cafe latte	3.50
Cafe mocha	3.50	Cappucino	3.25
Cafe au lait	2.75		

Teas
Chai with steamed milk 3.00
Chai with steamed chocolate 3.00
Ask your server for our list of fresh and dried leaf teas.

*We feature **Straus Organic Milk**
Soy milk is available   .50

17 % service charge for parties of six or more

FIGURE 4-14 Dessert Menu. *(Courtesy of Green's Restaurant, San Francisco, CA.)*

Review Questions

1. What is a prix fixe menu?

2. What is a semi à la carte menu?

3. Explain the principal characteristics of the special occasion menu.

4. Explain the characteristics of the luncheon menu.

5. What are the two types of banquet menus available, and how do they differ from one another?

6. What are the major characteristics of an institutional menu?

7. List the considerations that have to be kept in mind when you are planning an ethnic menu.

8. What is a specialty menu?

9. What are the elements that should be considered when you are designing a wine menu?

10. Discuss American, French, and modified Russian service.

Chapter 5

The Yield Test

Yield tests are an essential part of determining the profitability of a menu item. This chapter discusses the types of yield tests, how to do a yield test, and the importance of doing yield tests.

Objectives

1. To define yield tests
2. To explain how to use yield tests within the foodservice industry
3. To discuss how a yield test is used when you are planning menus
4. To calculate the cost of a yield test

Defining the Yield Test

A **yield test** is used to determine the amount of **edible product (EP)** (also referred to as yield) and the amount of **waste product (WP)** of a particular food item.

It is essential for the menu planner to know the amount of EP in food items so that the owner does not lose money by purchasing a food item that yields very little EP and produces WP that cannot be used. The higher a food item's yield is, the greater the portions that will be available and the higher the profit.

Yield tests should be done at least three times for every food item that is purchased in a foodservice operation. Management, chefs, and cooks should know how much each food item yields. Since foods have a wide variance in terms of their perishability, the amount of yield will differ from delivery to delivery. Food items such as meats, poultry, produce, fruits, and seafood that have a high perishability factor should have yield tests done on a regular basis.

Management must be demanding when setting specifications for food items. Specifications are factors that determine a standard of quality in a food product. Examples of such factors are

- Weight
- Color
- Shape
- Grade
- Texture
- Size
- Odor
- Packaging
- Product temperature
- Yield grade

It is these specifications that help to determine the quality of food.

A yield test should be done under two conditions: (1) in a controlled environment and (2) during actual production time. A **controlled environment** exists when the person who is conducting the yield test is not distracted by anything or anyone, is not rushed, and has all the necessary equipment to perform the yield test. Performing a yield test during actual production provides a **noncontrolled** environment where distractions exist.

The reason for conducting a yield test under both conditions is so that results from the yield test performed under a controlled environment will give management the maximum yield that the product can be expected to produce, whereas those from a yield test performed during the actual production period (a noncontrolled environment) will measure the actual yield accomplished. The actual yield accomplished is always lower until management trains the employees to cut and serve food items properly in order to gain a better yield.

Types of Yield Tests

There are two basic types of yield tests:

1. A convenience food yield test
2. A fresh food yield test

Convenience Food Yield Test

The **convenience food yield test** is done on food items that have been prepackaged into cans, bags, and boxes. This test consists of opening packages and weighing the amount of edible product. **Packing** is the extra filling placed inside a convenience food product to keep its quality.

This test will determine if the amount of packaging is within the specifications stated. If the amount of packing is not what the specifications state, then management is losing money by paying for excess packing. The Food and Drug Administration has set standards for the amount of packing to be used in all canned products.

Fresh Food Yield Test

The **fresh food yield test** (see Figure 5-1 for form) is done on food items that are purchased in an unaltered, fresh state. This test consists of weighing food items before starting any type of preparation and after completing the final preparation. This yield test is completed in eight steps, which are:

1. Weigh the fresh food product as it is received.
2. Weigh the fresh food product after it comes out of storage. Most foods will lose weight during storage through evaporation.
3. Trim any undesirable parts, such as fat, bones, outer leaves, and so on.
4. Wash and weigh the fresh food product. (At this point, the convenience food yield test also can be calculated in the same manner.)
5. Prepare and cook the food. Weigh the food to determine the amount of weight loss caused through shrinkage during the cooking stage.
6. Cut the food product into portion sizes.
7. Weigh the food product to determine the amount of edible product lost during the portioning or carving stage.
8. Once the food item has been cut into the total number of portions, total the amount of waste product.

Item_____ Grade_____ Date_____

Pieces_____ Weight_____ lb_____ oz Average Wt._____ lb_____oz

Total Cost $_____ at $_____ per_____ Purveyor_____

Breakdown	No.	Weight		Ratio to Total Weight	Value per Pound	Total Value	Cost of ea.		Portion		Cost Factor per	
		lb	oz				lb	oz	Size	Value	lb	Por.
Total												

$$\frac{\text{Cost Factor}}{\text{per lb or Portion}} = \frac{\text{Ready-to-Eat Value per lb or Portion}}{\text{Purchase Price per lb}}$$

Cooking Loss
To find ready-to-eat value of cuts at a new market price, multiply new price per lb by the cost factor.

Item_____

Portion Size_____ Cooked_____ hr_____ min at_____degrees

Portion Cost Factor_____ Cooked_____ hr_____ min at_____degrees

Breakdown	No.	Weight		Ratio to Total Weight	Value per Pound	Total Value	Ready-to-Eat Value per		Ready-to-Eat Portion		Cost Factor per	
		lb	oz				lb	oz	Size	Value	lb	Por.
Original Weight												
Loss in Trimming												
Trimmed Weight												
Loss in Cooking												
Cooked Weight												
Bones and Trim												
Loss in Slicing												
Salable Meat												

$$\frac{\text{Cost Factor}}{\text{per lb or Portion}} = \frac{\text{Ready-to-Eat Value per lb or Portion}}{\text{Purchase Price per lb}}$$

FIGURE 5-1 Yield Test Card.

Calculating a Yield Test

Step 1

Establish the AP weight. The **AP weight** is the as purchased weight of the raw product. Weigh the product.

Step 2

Calculate the amount of waste. Weigh all waste product, such as bones, fat, outer leaves, and so forth.

Step 3

Calculate the edible product.

$$\text{AP weight} - \text{Waste product} = \text{Edible product}$$

For example,

$$10 \text{ lb} - 3 \text{ lb} = 7 \text{ lb}$$

Step 4

Convert the edible product unit of measurement (possibly pounds to ounces), if the single portion size to be served is different from the edible product amount.

$$\text{Edible product} \times 16 \text{ oz (1 lb)} = \text{Total number of portions}$$

For example,

$$7 \text{ lb} \times 16 \text{ oz} = 112 \text{ oz}$$

Step 5

Calculate the number of individual portions available. Divide the total number of portions available by the individual portion size to get the number of portions available. For example,

$$112 \text{ oz} \div 4 \text{ oz} = 28$$

Step 6

Establish the individual portion cost. Take the total cost and divide it by the total number of portions. This equals the individual portion cost. For example,

$$\$20 \div 28 = \$0.72$$

 *Practice Problems*

1. AP weight   20 lb
    AP price $3.55 lb   Total Extension _____
    Waste   2 lb   Total Number of Portions _____
    Portion size 3 oz   Portion Cost _____

2. AP weight   30 lb   Total Extension _____
    AP price $4.25 lb   Total Number of Portions _____
    Waste   3 lb   Portion Cost _____
    Portion size 3 oz

3. AP weight   8 lb
    AP price $2.10 lb   Total Extension _____
    Waste   3 lb   Total Number of Portions _____
    Portion size 6 oz   Portion Cost _____

4. AP weight   22.5 lb
    AP price $1.95 lb   Total Extension _____
    Waste   3 oz   Total Number of Portions _____
    Portion size 4 oz   Portion Cost _____

5. AP weight   28 lb
    AP price $4.25 lb   Total Extension _____
    Waste   3 lb   Total Number of Portions _____
    Portion size 4 oz   Portion Cost _____

6. AP weight   45 lb
    AP price $1.25 lb   Total Extension _____
    Waste   3 lb   Total Number of Portions _____
    Portion size 6 oz   Portion Cost _____

7. AP weight   12 lb
    AP price $3.38 lb   Total Extension _____
    Waste   1.5 lb   Total Number of Portions _____
    Portion size 5 oz   Portion Cost _____

8. AP weight   33 lb
   AP price $2.78 lb   Total Extension _____
   Waste   2 lb   Total Number of Portions _____
   Portion size   8 oz   Portion Cost _____

9. AP weight   36 lb
   AP price $5.88 lb   Total Extension _____
   Waste   2 lb   Total Number of Portions _____
   Portion size   4 oz   Portion Cost _____

10. AP weight   78 lb
    AP price $4.88 lb   Total Extension _____
    Waste   12 oz   Total Number of Portions _____
    Portion size 6 oz   Portion Cost _____

The AP weight must be converted into ounces before you subtract the waste.

Answers to Practice Problems

1. Total extension is $71.00.
   Total number of portions is 96.
   Portion cost is $0.74.

2. Total extension is $127.50.
   Total number of portions is 144.
   Portion cost is $0.89.

3. Total extension is $16.80.
   Total number of portions is 13.3 (= 13).
   Portion cost is $1.26 (= $1.26).

4. Total extension is $43.88.
   Total number of portions is 89.25 (= 89).
   Portion cost is $0.49.

5. Total extension is $119.00.
   Total number of portions is 100.
   Portion cost is $1.19.

6. Total extension is $56.25.
   Total number of portions is 112.
   Portion cost is $0.50.

7. Total extension is $40.56.
   Total number of portions is 33.6.
   Portion cost is $1.21.

8. Total extension is $91.74.
   Total number of portions is 62.
   Portion cost is $1.48.

9. Total extension is $211.68.
   Total number of portions is 136.
   Portion cost is $1.56.

10. Total extension is $380.64.
    Total number of portions is 206.
    Portion cost is $1.85.

Edible Yields Percentage

The following edible yields information is prepared by the Nutritional and Technical Services Division and the Human Nutrition Information Service of the U.S. Department of Agriculture and the National Marine Fisheries Service of the U.S. Department of Commerce.

EDIBLE YIELDS PERCENTAGE AFTER COOKING

BEEF	ONE POUND AS PURCHASED = EDIBLE (COOKED) YIELD (%)
Brisket, corned (boned)	= 70%
Brisket, fresh (boned)	= 69%
Ground meats (26% fat)	= 72%
Ground meats (20% fat)	= 74%
Ground meats (15% fat)	= 75%
Ground meats (10% fat)	= 76%
Roast, chuck (without bone)	= 63%
Roast, chuck (with bone)	= 54%
Rump (without bone)	= 68%
Rump (with bone)	= 62%
Steak, flank	= 73%
Steak, round (without bone)	= 63%
Stew meat	= 61%

POULTRY	ONE POUND AS PURCHASED = EDIBLE (COOKED) YIELD (%)
Chicken breast halves (approx. 6.1 oz with ribs)	= 66% w/skin
	= 56% w/o skin
Chicken breast halves (approx. 7.5 oz with backs)	= 55% w/skin
	= 47% w/o skin
Turkey	= 53% w/skin
Turkey	= 47% w/o skin

OTHER MEATS

Lamb chops (shoulder, with bone)	=	46%
Lamb roast (leg, without bone)	=	61%
Lamb roast (shoulder, without bone)	=	54%
Lamb stew meat	=	65%
Veal cutlets	=	54%
Pork chops, loin	=	54%
Pork roast (leg, without bone)	=	57%
Pork roasts (leg, with bone)	=	46%
Pork loin (without bone)	=	58%
Pork loin (with bone)	=	45%
Shoulder/boston butt (without bone)	=	60%
Shoulder/boston butt (with bone)	=	52%
Shoulder/picnic (without bone)	=	57%
Shoulder/picnic (with bone)	=	42%
Canadian bacon	=	69%
Ham (without bone)	=	63%
Ham (with bone)	=	53%

FRESH VEGETABLES AND FRUITS	ONE POUND AS PURCHASED	=	EDIBLE YIELD (%)
Apples		=	91%
Apricots		=	93%
Asparagus		=	53%
Avocados		=	67%
Bananas		=	65%
Beans, green		=	88%
Beans, lima		=	44%
Beans, wax (yellow)		=	88%
Beet greens		=	48%
Beets		=	77%
Broccoli		=	81%
Brussels sprouts		=	76%
Cabbage		=	87%
Cabbage, red		=	64%
Cantaloupe		=	52%

FRESH VEGETABLES AND FRUITS	ONE POUND AS PURCHASED	=	EDIBLE YIELD (%)
Carrots		=	70%
Cauliflower		=	62%
Celery		=	83%
Chard, Swiss		=	92%
Cherries		=	98%
Chicory		=	89%
Collards		=	57%
Corn, on the cob		=	33%
Cranberries		=	95%
Cucumbers		=	84%
Eggplant		=	81%
Endive, escarole		=	78%
Grapefruit		=	52%
Grapes		=	97%

Honeydew melon	=	46%
Kale	=	67%
Lemons	=	43% (3/4 c juice)
Lettuce, head	=	76%
Lettuce, leaf	=	66%
Lettuce, romaine	=	64%
Limes	=	47% (7/8 c juice)

FRESH VEGETABLES AND FRUITS	ONE POUND AS PURCHASED	=	EDIBLE YIELD (%)
Mangoes	=		69%
Mushrooms	=		98%
Mustard greens	=		93%
Nectarines	=		91%
Okra	=		87%
Onions, green	=		83%
Onions	=		88%
Oranges	=		71%
Papaya	=		67%
Parsley	=		92%
Parsnips	=		83%
Peaches	=		76%
Pears	=		92%
Peas, green	=		38%
Peppers, green	=		80%
Pineapple	=		54%
Plantains, ripe	=		65%
Plums	=		94%
Potatoes, white	=		81%
Pumpkin	=		70%
Radishes	=		94%

FRESH VEGETABLES AND FRUITS	ONE POUND AS PURCHASED	=	EDIBLE YIELD (%)
Raspberries	=		96%
Rhubarb	=		86%
Rutabagas	=		85%
Spinach	=		88%
Squash, summer	=		95%
Squash, zucchini	=		94%
Squash acorn	=		70%
Squash, butternut	=		84%
Squash, Hubbard	=		64%
Strawberries	=		88%
Sweet potatoes	=		80%
Tangerines	=		74%
Tomatoes	=		99%
Tomatoes, cherry	=		97%
Turnips	=		70%
Watercress	=		92%
Watermelon	=		57%

Review Questions

1. Define yield test.

2. What do the following abbreviations mean: EP, AP, and WP?

3. What is the formula for finding a portion cost?

4. List five types of waste that can be produced during a yield test.

Additional Readings

Jack E. Miller and David V. Pavesic, *Menu Pricing and Strategy,* 4th ed. (New York: Wiley & Sons, 1996).

Arno Schmidt, *Chef's Book of Formulas, Yields, and Sizes.* (New York: John Wiley & Sons, 1990).

Software Packages

"Chef's Calculators," from *The Book of Yields,* by Francis T. Lynch: www.chefdesk.com

"ExecuChef,™" by Susan Schaeffer: www.ExecuChef.com

Chapter 6

Standard Recipes

$\mathcal{S}$tandard recipes are needed to produce a standard-quality food product. This chapter discusses a variety of methods for writing recipes, different techniques for standardizing recipes, and the importance of standardizing recipes.

 Objectives

1. To give the student an understanding of the importance of using standardized recipes
2. To show standard recipe card format
3. To identify the elements of a recipe card
4. To illustrate different methods of recipe creativity

Defining Standard Recipes in the Industry

A **standard recipe** is the only recipe used to prepare a particular menu item. The objective of writing, maintaining, and using standardized recipes is to consistently guarantee the customer a quality product.

When customers enjoy what they eat at a restaurant, they want to repeat the experience of eating those foods. Customers expect the food quality to be as good as (or better than) the quality they most recently experienced when they ate at the foodservice operation. A foodservice operation that does not duplicate the same food quality every time the product is made and served will disappoint its customers. In today's competitive world, customers will not tolerate inconsistent food quality from a foodservice operation. Customers expect the best quality of food that their money can buy, and competition demands that the foodservice operation meet those expectations or be left behind in competition. By standardizing recipes, the foodservice operation is able to meet customers' demands and remain competitive in the foodservice industry. Therefore, in terms of profit, a foodservice operation cannot afford to disappoint its customers by serving an inconsistent product.

The fast-food industry, with its standards of quick service, low prices, and organized systems to produce a consistent quality of foods, has taught the foodservice industry and the consumer the value of producing a standardized food product. To set a standard means to adapt food quality to a level or degree of excellence. The standardizing of recipes is one of the first steps that must be taken to obtain the level of excellence that customers come to expect. Some smaller foodservice operations do not use standardized recipe cards per se, because the expense of writing, testing, and recording the recipes on index cards or in computer files is too great for most smaller operations. Hotels, institutions, foodservice chains, and larger restaurants use standardized recipes and systems because they can afford the expense and do realize the value of having standardized recipes.

Chefs and/or cooks should know how to produce the items on the menu, and management should have knowledge of how food items on the menu are prepared. If a chef and/or a cook cannot be at work, management must often take over. If management is not familiar with the preparation and cannot fill in for a chef or a cook, the food quality will not be consistent, causing customer dissatisfaction, loss of sales, and perhaps a damaged reputation.

There are different formats for recording recipes. Recipes can be written on plain sheets of paper or on index cards, or they can be placed in computer files. The format you select needs to be based on the system that is going to provide the best support for your operation. When using standardized recipes, you must remember to do the following:

- Ensure that there are no errors within the recipe.
- Test and retest them to achieve the excellence of food quality desired.
- Keep them simple to read and to follow.
- Check to be sure that the recipes are grammatically correct.
- Use them.

Management should select a standardized recipe card system that is going to fit its operation. A simple system will be more useful and therefore more successful than a complex one. Standard recipes can be used most effectively when you are training cooks and management personnel.

All food items are to be tested and retested for food quality, cost, and ease of preparation before they are placed on the menu. When these tests have been accomplished, the recipe should be recorded in a manner that is grammatically correct, easy to read, and simple to follow.

Recording Recipes

A recipe card (see Figure 6-1) should include the following information:

- Name of the recipe (item to be made)
- Yield (total portions and/or number of servings)
- Portion size
- Index number for identification purposes
- Ingredients column
- Weight column
- Measurement column
- Directions or method of preparation column
- Picture of the finished product

Item _____		Menu Number _____	
Portions Size _____		Issue Number _____	
Yield _____			
Ingredients	Weight	Measure	Method of Preparation

FIGURE 6-1 Recipe Card Format.

It can be expensive to place a picture of the finished product with each recipe. However, the saying that a picture is worth a thousand words carries a lot of truth. It is much easier to train a cook or a manager to prepare a recipe if the person has a picture in mind of how the finished product will look. Any presentation mistakes can be identified by referring to the recipe picture and corrected before the customer receives the menu item.

The weight column refers only to ingredients that are expressed by ounces and pounds. The measure column refers to all other terms of measurement, such as taste, pinch, dash, teaspoons, tablespoons, cups, pints, quarts, gallons, and number 2 or number 10 cans. The direction or method of preparation column must be written in a clear, grammatically correct way, with simple steps to follow. To save time for the chef or cook, always list prerequisite tasks first (for example, preheating the oven). Proceed with a step-by-step method for preparing the recipe (see Figures 6-2 and 6-3).

Item New England Clam Chowder			Recipe Number S-1
Portion Size 8-oz bowl			Portions 8
Yield ½ gallon			
Ingredients	Weight	Measure	Method of Preparation
Shucked clams	1	quart	A. Drain clams, saving the juice.
Chopped bacon	8	tablespoons	Chop clams.
Sliced onions	1	cup	B. Cook bacon in a saucepan
Diced potatoes	3½	cups	until crisp. Do not drain grease.
Salt	½	teaspoon	Add onions and brown slightly.
Pepper		pinch	C. Add potatoes, salt, pepper,
Hot water	2	cups	and water. Cook for 10 minutes.
Milk	1	quart	D. Add clams, milk, Half and Half,
Half and Half	1	cup	and clam juice; cook until the
Soda crackers	8	each	potatoes are tender, about 10
			minutes. Do not overcook the
			potatoes.
			E. Pour chowder over crackers
			in serving bowls.

FIGURE 6-2 New England Clam Chowder Recipe.

| Menu Item <u>Roast leg of lamb</u> | | Recipe Number <u>E-2</u> |
| Portion Size <u>6 oz</u> | | Portions <u>8</u> |
Ingredients	Quantity	Method of Preparation

Leg of lamb, bone in
Olive oil
Dried rosemary
Garlic seasoning
Salt and pepper
 	
Chicken stock
 	
Fresh mint sprig
and or mint jelly
	6 pounds
	2 tablespoons (1 ounce)
	1 tablespoon (½ ounce)
	1 tablespoon (½ ounce)
	2 tablespoons (1 ounce)
	
	1/3 cup
		Preheat oven to 325°F.
		A. Place lamb on a rack in a shallow roasting plan.
		B. Brush olive oil over lamb.
		C. Rub rosemary, garlic, salt, and pepper onto lamb.
		D. Roast for 3 hours or to an internal temperature of 155–165 degrees for medium. Do not cover lamb while it is cooking. Allow roast to stand 10–15 minutes, and then carve and serve.
		   Deglaze the roasting pan by adding the chicken broth to the drippings in the pan. Bring to a simmer, stirring to loosen caramelized drippings on the bottom of the pan. Ladle glaze over sliced lamb.
		   Garnish by placing a sprig or a dollop of mint onto each plate.

FIGURE 6-3 Roast Leg of Lamb Recipe.

Recipe Creativity

To be competitive in the foodservice industry, it is vital that foodservice operations provide the types of food that customers demand. Since customer food preferences are always changing, the foodservice operation must constantly offer different foods. Therefore, foodservice operations should change their menus often. The more profitable restaurants arouse their customers' curiosity by regularly preparing new and exciting dishes (perhaps as often as weekly) to tantalize their tastes. Successful foodservice operations experiment with recipes on a regular basis, not only when they are changing the menu.

One method of helping to create sales as well as adding excitement to creating menus is to experiment. First take a recipe and prepare the recipe according to the directions. Then make it a second time and change a few ingredients or the amounts of ingredients so that it becomes your way of making the recipe. Give the recipe to other cooks and tell them to prepare it, first as is, then your way, and finally, their own way. When this process is complete, you will have a recipe with three different variations. Next, have your employees taste the product and evaluate it. Listen to your employees' suggestions and make changes if necessary.

Once the employees are excited about the product, start giving samples to a few customers each night. Ask the customers what they think of the product and how it might be improved. Allowing employees and customers to get directly involved in the planning and creating of menu items gives them a vested interest in the foodservice operation. Do this for about a month in order to get the customers and employees talking about the new food product. After everyone is talking about the product, have your employees verbally suggest it to customers when they are describing the nightly special. *Do not place this product on the menu (verbal sales only)!* Wait until the product has become a good seller (e.g., you achieve 15–20 percent of sales for a night) to place it on the menu. Not placing this product on the menu immediately keeps the anticipation level high and adds to the excitement when the item actually appears on the menu.

Review Questions

1. Why is it important to standardize recipes?

2. Which sector of the foodservice industry does a particularly good job in producing a standardized food product?

3. List three rules in making standardized recipes successful.

4. Name the items that are necessary on a standardized recipe card.

5. How do standardizing recipes increase the quality of menu items?

Additional Readings

Clement Ojugo, *Practical Food and Beverage Cost Control.* (Albany, NY: Delmar Publisher, 1999).

Nancy Scanlon, *Marketing by Menu,* 3rd ed. (New York: John Wiley & Sons, 1999).

Chapter 7

Recipe Costing

Objectives

1. To explain why recipe costing is necessary

2. To identify different methods of lowering the food cost percentage

3. To identify the elements in costing out a recipe

4. To illustrate how to cost out a recipe

Recipe Costing

Recipe costing is the method used to determine the profit on food products. This chapter discusses the importance of costing out recipes, the methodology used to cost out recipes, and examples of costing out recipes.

Assigning the Task of Recipe Costing

The majority of people who enter the foodservice industry do so to make a profit. The costing out of recipes is vital in generating a profit.

The task of costing out recipes is not difficult to understand. Although it is a very time-consuming task, the expense of costing out recipes is well worth the investment. To accomplish this task, management needs to assign a person who is responsible for overseeing the project from start to finish. This individual may not be the only person responsible for the entire project; however, this individual is responsible for the completion of the task, which includes a complete analysis of the recipe costing system.

It has been found that, when a group of people or a committee is assigned the task of costing out recipes for a foodservice operation, the task rarely gets accomplished. Therefore, assigning one person to be the leader or coordinator usually works best. This person should have a clear understanding of how recipe costing relates to food costing and profit, and of the importance of this task.

The Importance of Recipe Costing

Why is recipe costing necessary? To understand the full effect that recipe costing has on the amount of profit that a foodservice operation is going to make, you must first understand the relationship between food cost and profit.

To obtain and maintain maximum profit, a foodservice operation needs to be aware of expenses. The four major expenses are:

1. Food
2. Labor
3. Overhead
4. Profit

Food expense is the cost of the food being purchased. Some foodservice operations include beverages in this category. **Labor expense** is the total cost of the labor force that a food service operation employs. **Overhead expense** is defined as all other expenses except food, labor, and profit. Examples of overhead expenses are the cost of equipment, uniforms, laundry service, water, electricity, rent or mortgage, and taxes. **Profit** is considered to be an accrual expense before any cash flow or sales. It takes money to make money. Only after a sales transaction has taken place, all expenses have been paid, and there is money left over in the cash register is there a profit. At that time, the profit is no longer considered to be an expense but rather an asset to the foodservice operation.

Once a cash flow has been established, the relationship of the three other expenses—food, labor, and overhead—to profit becomes inverse. **Inverse relationship** means that, when one of the expenses increases or decreases, it affects the profit inversely. For example, when the cost of food, labor, and overhead decrease, profit increases. The three major expense categories, plus profit, must equal 100 percent. Sales at 100 percent represent all the money that a foodservice operation can possibly make.

It is important for the management team to establish an annual forecast of its sales, profit, and expenses. The management team must keep track of all of these on a daily, weekly, and monthly basis in order to obtain the projected annual profit. The management team cannot wait three or six months from the opening date to see if it is making a profit. If management is not making a profit, it will not take three months to recognize this fact. Even if a profit is being made, there is still the need to evaluate the profit to see if it is up to the projected amount.

Most small family and independent foodservice operations are concerned primarily that there is enough money in the cash register at the end of the day to pay bills and to still make a profit. There is nothing wrong with this philosophy, as long as the family is still interested in increasing daily profits. By simply understanding and implementing greater control of the three expense areas, this goal is possible.

Here are six guidelines to achieving a greater profit:

- Do comparative buying. Purchase food from more than two purveyors or vendors. Occasionally, purchase food from your regular purveyor's competition. Doing so will keep your relationship with your regular purveyor honest, and he or she will try harder to keep you as a satisfied customer.

- Do not always purchase a product with the lowest price. Never sacrifice your quality standards. The quality of the food that you serve is determined by management. Your customers will appreciate and will pay a higher price for a quality food product. When you compromise quality and charge the same price, customers will disapprove.

- Pilferage is the biggest contributor to a high food cost percentage. Employees oftentimes do not fully understand the implications of eating a food product without paying for it. The management team must decide what type of meal policy it wants to implement and how to enforce it. The real problem is that employees in the foodservice industry will eat in the walk-in refrigerator whenever management lets them do so. Placing a lock on the walk-in when it is not being used and restricting its access to the cooks can help control this problem. It is impossible to keep all employees from snacking or eating at the foodservice operation, but management must be aware of the effect of this problem on profit when it is not controlled.

- Proper training of all employees will help reduce food cost. Food can be wasted because of employee accidents. The cook who burns the Lobster Newburgh, the service personnel who spill the sauce, and the bartender who incorrectly mixes a drink all contribute to an increase in the food cost percentage. Most accidents occur when people become careless about what they are doing. A proper training program teaches employees to take pride and care in their work. The greater the pride employees have in their work, the more care they are going to take in doing their jobs. Thus, accidents will be reduced.

- Portioning food in its proper portion size is vital in controlling the food cost percentage. When a cook serves an extra 2 or 3 ounces of a food product, it increases the food cost percentage. When the customer is receiving more and paying less, the food cost that management has costed out will not be accurate.
- Waste of food caused by overproduction is another factor that contributes to less profit. For controls on accurate forecasting, see Chapter 9, "Sales History."

How to Cost Out a Recipe

Once a recipe has been selected, it needs to be recorded in a format that is easy to use for costing out recipes. (See Figure 7-1 for an example.) The form should contain the following information:

A. Recipe name

B. Recipe identification number

C. Portion size

D. Yield or number of portions

E. Ingredients

F. Waste percentage

G. Edible portion (EP)

H. As purchased (AP)

I. Unit purchase price

J. Conversion measure

K. Ingredient cost

L. Preliminary subtotal recipe cost

M. Q factor of 1 percent (place percentage in this box and then multiply the Q factor % by the preliminary subtotal recipe cost)

N. Q factor cost

O. Subtotal recipe cost (add Q factor cost to the preliminary subtotal recipe cost)

P. Portion cost (divide the subtotal recipe cost by the total portions/yield)

Q. Additional cost (if this is an à la carte menu item, leave this box blank; if not, place the portion cost of the other menu items in this box.)

R. Total recipe cost (add portion cost with any additional cost; if there are none, then the portion cost becomes the total recipe cost)

S. Desired overall food cost percentage (retrieve this number from the annual profit and loss statement)

T. Preliminary selling price (divide the total recipe cost by the desired food cost percentage)

U. Adjusted/Actual selling price (based on what the customer is willing to pay)

V. Adjusted/Actual food cost percentage (divide the total recipe cost by the adjusted/actual selling price)

Recipe Heading

The recipe heading includes **A. Recipe Name, B. Recipe Identification Number, C. Portion Size,** and **D. Yield.**

A. Recipe Name. Indicate the recipe name here. If the name is in a foreign language, include its English translation.

B. Recipe Identification Number. Give each recipe an identification number so that the recipes can be organized in an easy, organized method.

C. Portion Size. Indicate the portion size here. The portion size is the amount of food or beverage that the customer will be served.

D. Yield. The yield is the quantity of edible food or beverage that the recipe will make.

Column E: Ingredients

List the ingredients in this column.

Column F: Waste Percentage

Most recipes call for ingredients that are 100 percent edible, that is, having no waste. The fact is, however, that most fresh food products, such as poultry, fish, seafood, and produce, have a certain percentage of waste.

The cook must calculate the amount of waste that a product has in order to accurately order the amount of food needed. For example, in

A Recipe Name _____					**B** Recipe ID No. _____	
C Portion Size _____						
D Yield _____						

E Ingredients	**F** Waste %	**G** EP	**H** AP	**I** Unit Purchase Price	**J** Conversion Measure	**K** Ingredient Cost

L Subtotal	
M Q Factor %	
N Q Factor $	
O Subtotal Recipe Cost	
P Portion Cost	
Q Additional Cost	
R Total Recipe Cost	
S Desired Food Cost %	
T Preliminary Selling Price	
U Adjusted/ Actual Selling Price	
V Adjusted/ Actual Food Cost %	

FIGURE 7-1 Recipe Costing Form.

Figure 7-2, the recipe calls for 3 pounds of 100 percent edible round steak, the cook must take into account the fact that a piece of round steak usually will have excess fat on it that has to be trimmed. If the cook does not take this into consideration before purchasing the meat, then he or she will end up with less than 3 pounds of meat, thus altering the yield of the recipe and leaving the cook with six portions short.

To calculate the amount of round steak needed for the recipe to yield six portions, the cook must establish the amount of waste that the round steak will produce. This is done by conducting a yield test on the round steak. A yield test will give the amount of edible product (EP) and the amount of waste product (WP).

Column G: Edible Product Amount (EP)

The Edible Product (EP) column shows the amount of the ingredient in the recipe excluding the waste.

Column H: As Purchased Amount (AP)

The As Purchased (AP) column is used to indicate the amount of the ingredient in the recipe including the waste product. This amount is what is purchased from the purveyor.

When only the AP amount is given or needed, it is not necessary to calculate the waste product. An example is the amount of salt needed in a recipe. There is no waste product in salt.

The round steak has a waste of 3 percent and an EP amount of 3 pounds. To find the amount of round steak that needs to be purchased (AP amount), the cook must use the following formula (W = waste):

$$AP = \frac{EP \times 100}{100\% - W\%}$$

The waste amount is put into the formula as a whole number:

$$AP = \frac{3 \times 100}{100 - 3} = \frac{300}{97} = 3.09 \text{ lbs}$$

The actual amount of round steak that the cook needs to purchase is 3.09 pounds. The 0.09, or 9 percent, represents 9 percent of a pound (16 ounces), which is:

$$0.09 \times 16 = 1.44 \text{ oz } (1\frac{1}{2} \text{ ozs})$$

E Ingredients	F Waste %	G EP	H AP	I Unit Purchase Price	J Conversion Measure	K Ingredient Cost
A Recipe Name <u>Swiss Steak in Sour Cream</u>					B Recipe ID No. <u>E-1</u>	
C Portion Size <u>8 oz</u>						
D Yield <u>6 servings</u>						

E Ingredients	F Waste %	G EP	H AP	I Unit Purchase Price	J Conversion Measure	K Ingredient Cost
Round steak	3	3 lb	3.09	$2.59 lb		$8.00
Salt			½ tsp	$1.85 lb	$\frac{0.50\ tsp}{96\ tsp} = 0.005$	$0.01
Pepper	Q factor		¼ tsp			Q factor
Paprika			1 tsp	$1.80 lb	$\frac{1\ tsp}{96\ tsp} = 0.010$	$0.02
Flour			½ c	$2.00 lb	$\frac{0.5\ c}{2\ c} = 0.25$	$0.50
Chopped onion	12	½ cup	4.55 oz	$0.18 lb	4.55 oz = 0.284	$0.05
Sour cream			½ c	$0.89 pt	$\frac{0.5\ c}{2\ c} = 0.25$	$0.23
Boiling water						Q factor
Chopped parsley			¼ c	$0.55 lb	$\frac{2\ oz}{16\ oz} = 0.125$	$0.07

J Conversion Measure

Salt $\dfrac{0.50\ tsp}{96\ tsp} = 0.005$

Paprika $\dfrac{1\ tsp}{96\ tsp} = 0.010$

Flour $\dfrac{0.50\ c}{2\ c} = 0.25$

Chopped onions $\dfrac{4.555\ oz}{16\ oz} = 0.284$

Sour cream $\dfrac{0.50\ c}{2\ c} = 0.25$

Chopped parsley $\dfrac{2\ oz}{16\ oz} = 0.125$

L Subtotal — $8.88
M Q factor (1%) multiply — × 0.01
N The subtotal equals $0.09 — $0.09
O Subtotal recipe cost equals the subtotal plus the $0.09 — $8.88 / +0.09 / $8.97
P Portion cost equals subtotal recipe cost divided by the recipe yield
$8.97 ÷ 6 = $1.50
Q Additional costs are added (there are no additional costs for this recipe)
R Total recipe cost — $1.50
Portion cost + additional cost
$1.50 + 0 = $1.50
S Desired food cost % — $0.40
T Preliminary selling price equals portion cost divided by the food cost % — $1.50 ÷ $0.40 = $3.75
U Actual selling price — $3.95
V Actual food cost % equals portion cost divided by the actual selling price
$1.50 ÷ $3.95 = $0.38 (38%)

FIGURE 7-2 Recipe Costing for Swiss Steak in Sour Cream.

A cook should shop around for a meat purveyor who will accept the exact specifications for the round steaks. There are purveyors who will cut meat to any specifications desired. You will pay an additional fee for the service, so, therefore, you should figure out which method is more profitable.

One way of recovering the extra cost of the waste is to use it in another food product. For example, the fat trimmed from the round steak can be rendered down and used in sautéing other food products, thus cutting down the amount of oil to be purchased for sautéing. The goal is to recover the additional cost in any way that is possible to help maintain a lower food cost. Another alternative is to increase menu prices.

Column I: Conversion Measure

The unit purchase price column lists the amount that the cook pays a purveyor for an ingredient.

Column J: Unit Purchase Price Column

The conversion measure column is where the conversion formula and the converting factor are written. The AP amount is often expressed in ounces, whereas the AP price is expressed in pounds. When there are two different units of measurement used, one of them must be converted so that both of them are the same. For example, in Figure 7-2, the chopped onions require an AP amount of 4.55 ounces, but very often they are purchased by the pound. In this recipe, onions are purchased at a unit price of $0.18 per pound. The question is, "How much do 4.55 ounces cost if onions are purchased at $0.18 per pound?" The menu planner cannot divide $0.18 by 4.55 ounces. To arrive at the correct answer, the menu planner first must find out what percentage 4.55 ounces is of 1 pound (16 ounces). This is done by dividing 4.55 ounces by 16 ounces, which equals a decimal-converting factor of 0.284. This 0.284 is the equivalent of 4.55 ounces. Now that the same unit of measurement is expressed in decimals, the onion conversion factor (0.284) times the unit price ($0.18) will equal the ingredient cost of $0.051 ($0.05).

Column K: Ingredient Cost

The ingredient cost column is used to note the total cost of the ingredient used in the recipe. The converting factor and the unit price are multiplied to arrive at this figure. All of the ingredient costs in column K are added together to calculate a subtotal recipe cost, which is then written in column L, the subtotal recipe cost column.

Column L: Subtotal of the Recipe Cost

Write the sum of all of the ingredient costs from column K in column L. This is the subtotal of the recipe cost column.

Column M: Q Factor %

The **Q factor** is the price that the cook must charge to recover the cost of all of the ingredients that are too minor to calculate. For example, when a recipe calls for a dash or a pinch of an ingredient, this amount becomes too difficult to cost out, especially since the amount that a cook uses in a pinch or a dash will differ from time to time.

One method that is used to recover the cost of a minor ingredient is to use a percentage factor. Since the amount of the ingredient to be used in this situation is questionable, we call this recovering cost factor a Q factor (Q stands for questionable).

The percentage amount of 1 percent is based on the following:

1. Most recipes do not have more than three Q factors in them.
2. The cost of these Q factor ingredients does not add up to 1 percent of the subtotal of the recipe.

Thus it is important that the menu planner be selective when he or she is deciding on the Q factor. The exception to using more than 1 percent of the recipe subtotal would be if the ingredient were expensive, such as saffron.

Column N: Q Factor in Dollars

The monetary value of the Q factor is calculated by multiplying the recipe subtotal by 1 percent. The answer is written in this column.

Column O: Subtotal Recipe Cost

The subtotal recipe cost is calculated by adding the monetary value of the Q factor to the subtotal recipe cost. The answer is written in this column.

Column P: Portion Cost

To calculate the portion cost (PC), divide the subtotal recipe cost by the total number of portions that the recipe yields.

Column Q: Additional Costs

When a food item is to be sold as a semi à la carte item, the portion cost of any additional food items are cost out separately and are written in this column. For example, in Figure 7-2, the Swiss Steak in Sour Cream comes with a baked potato and green peas. The menu planner calculates the portion cost of the baked potato and the green peas separately. The cost of these items are added to the recipe subtotal cost column (column O), which determines the total recipe cost (column R). Another way of expressing the total recipe cost is by adding all of the costs of food items on the plate.

If customers are given a choice of a vegetable or starch, the menu planner must add to the cost of the entrée the highest-priced vegetable or starch. For example, most menus offer a choice of baked, mashed, or French fried potatoes with an entrée. The menu planner must cost out all three potato dishes in order to decide which one will be added to the portion cost of the entrée. The menu planner should not offer the customer a choice of vegetables that vary greatly in cost. Select vegetables that are similar in price in order to avoid having to charge too much for the entrée.

Column R: Total Recipe Cost (Plate Cost)

The total recipe cost is calculated by adding the portion cost (column P) and the additional costs (column Q). This will give you the cost of the food being placed on the plate.

Column S: Desired Overall Food Cost Percentage

The desired overall food cost percentage is determined by management. The percentage is based on the annual food cost percentage that management desires to achieve in order to make the projected annual profit. The percentage will vary according to the foodservice concept and the annual profit and loss statement.

Column T: Preliminary Selling Price

The preliminary selling price is established by dividing the total recipe cost (column R) by the desired overall food cost percentage (column S). It is called a preliminary selling price because most likely it is not the actual selling price that will be placed on the sales menu. It is the first price arrived at by maintaining a determined food cost percentage.

Column U: Adjusted Actual Selling Price

The actual selling price is the selling price at which the product will be sold on the menu. This price will differ from the preliminary selling price, because it is based on the dollar amount that the customer is willing to pay for the product. Other factors that influence the actual selling price are

- Direct competition's price for the food product
- Demand (popularity) of the food product
- Availability of the food product

The menu planner must examine all three factors before adjusting the preliminary selling price.

Column V: Adjusted Actual Food Cost Percentage

Once the actual selling price has been readjusted either up or down, the menu planner can calculate the actual food cost percentage. This process is accomplished by dividing the total recipe cost (column R) by the actual selling price (column U).

The main objective for the menu planner in costing out recipes is to accurately calculate the cost of the food and to mark up the total recipe cost price to pay for labor cost and overhead cost, and to make a profit. The menu planner has to adjust the preliminary selling price to an actual selling price, which sometimes means lowering the profit margin made on the food product. If the preliminary selling price of barbeque chicken wings is $3.50, for example, and the chicken wings will not sell at that price because the customers will think that the price is too high or because the competition is selling chicken wings at $3, the price must be lowered in order to make the sale and to assure customer satisfaction. The problem, however, is that this product is not making the profit needed to reach the annual projected profit margin. The menu planner must, therefore, compensate for the lower profit margin on the chicken wings. A way of recovering the $0.55 difference is to spread out the cost throughout the menu. This is known as **balancing the menu.**

Menus have a certain number of high food cost items and a certain number of low food cost items. Every foodservice operation would like to have only low food cost items on the menu in order to generate a better profit. Unfortunately, low food cost items are not always the choice of the majority of customers. Prime rib of beef is not the highest profit item on most menus, but it is one of the most popular choices. Keeping some high food cost items on the menu is necessary to keep patrons. However, it is also necessary for a foodservice operation to maintain a good balance on the menu between high and low food cost items in order to maintain a healthy profit margin.

Review Questions

1. What does EP and AP have to do with recipe costing?

2. What are three methods of lowering a food cost percentage?

3. Why is recipe costing necessary?

4. Define Q factor, and explain how it is used in the costing out of a recipe.

5. Explain how *balancing a menu* is done.

Additional Readings

Jack E. Miller and David V. Pavesic, *Menu Pricing and Strategy,* 4th ed. (New York: Wiley & Sons, 1996).

Paul R. Dittmer and Gerald G. Griffin, *Principles of Food, Beverage, and Labor Cost Controls.* (New York: John Wiley & Sons, 1999).

Chapter 8

Characteristics of a Menu

*O*nce the menu has been costed out and final decisions have been made concerning food selection, the menu planner can begin to plan the organization and presentation of the menu. Decisions concerning paper, print, color, listing of items, size, and the cover design must be made. It is important that the menu planner have a basic knowledge about these menu mechanics in order to facilitate communication with a printer and achieve the best results.

Balance, variety, composition, and descriptive copy of food and beverage items, truth-in-menu, and menu labeling also should be considered before the menu planner sends materials to the printer. The characteristics of a menu will be discussed at length in this chapter.

 *Objectives*

1. To introduce and explain the characteristics of a menu, which include paper, print, color, balance, variety, composition, descriptive copy, truth-in-menu, menu labeling, listing of items, size, and cover design

2. To show how careful attention to menu presentation can help to merchandise menu items more effectively

The menu planner must pay careful attention to the following items when he or she is preparing a menu:

- Paper
- Print
- Color
- Balance
- Variety
- Composition
- Descriptive copy
- Truth-in-menu
- Menu labeling
- Listing of items
- Size
- Cover design

Paper

To begin the process of designing a menu, the menu planner selects the quality of paper desired. When choosing the paper, the menu planner must keep in mind how frequently the menu will be used. If the menu is going to be changed daily, then a paper that is less expensive and less durable, uncoated, and lightweight can be chosen. On the other hand, a menu that does not change often would require a durable, coated, heavy stock, water-resistant, and stain-resistant paper. Durability is also an important consideration when the menu planner is selecting the paper for a cover.

When choosing paper, the menu planner must weigh the following factors:

- Strength
- Texture
- Color
- Opacity (**Opacity** refers to the property of paper, which minimizes the "show-through" of printing to the back side of a sheet of paper.)

Print

The print on a menu should be easy to read. It is vital that the print on a menu be sufficiently large.

There are various styles of type. We will discuss the three major ones: roman, modern, and script. **Roman type** is characterized by a combination of thin and thick characteristics. It is easy to read and is used in newspapers, magazine articles, and books. Roman type should be used in the descriptive copy on the menu (see Figure 8-1).

Modern type does not have the thick and thin characteristics that are found in Roman type. Its letters are thick block letters (see Figure 8-1). Many government buildings use modern print on exterior signs. Modern type can be used for headings and subheadings on the menu.

Script type looks like handwriting. Script is difficult to read and should be used only for headings or subheadings on the menu (see Figure 8-1). Headings on the menu might be Appetizers, Soups, Salads, Entrées, and Desserts. Subheadings might consist of the names of the items offered, such as Stuffed Mushrooms for an appetizer or Sirloin Steak with Hollandaise Sauce for an entrée.

The menu planner must also decide on the type size. **Type size** is measured in points, starting with 6 points and going up to 192 points (see Figure 8-2). Most menus should be done in at least 12 point type. Smaller type is too difficult to read. For the descriptive copy, space between lines must be allowed, called **leading.** Leading is also measured in points (see Figure 8-3). When there is no space between lines, this

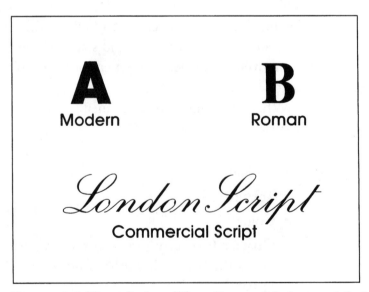

FIGURE 8-1 Three Styles of Type: Roman, Modern, and Script.

E 192 PT.   **E** 180 PT.   **E** 144 PT.   **E** 120 PT.

E 96 PT.   **E** 84 PT.   **E** 72 PT.   **E** 60 PT.   **E** 48 PT.

E 42 PT.   **E** 36 PT.   **E** 30 PT.   **E** 24 PT.   **E** 20 PT.   **E** 18 PT.

E 16 PT.   **E** 14 PT.   **E** 12 PT.   **E** 10 PT.   **E** 8 PT.   **E** 6 PT.

FIGURE 8-2 Examples of Point Sizes.

is referred to as **set solid.** It is important that the style of type be appropriate for the style of the restaurant. If the restaurant is modern, the menu should be modern as well.

The color of the type is also important. The type on a menu should be dark, and the background should be light. A light blue background with dark blue type often is very attractive. When the type is white and

Samples of Leading

■ Solid

>   Bananas Foster… A Brennan creation and now World Famous! Bananas
>   sautéed in butter, brown sugar, cinnamon and banana liqueur, then flamed
>   in rum. Served over vanilla ice cream. Scandalously Delicious!

■ 1-Point Leading

>   Bananas Foster… A Brennan creation and now World Famous! Bananas
>   sautéed in butter, brown sugar, cinnamon and banana liqueur, then flamed
>   in rum. Served over vanilla ice cream. Scandalously Delicious!

■ 2-Point Leading

>   Bananas Foster… A Brennan creation and now World Famous! Bananas
>   sautéed in butter, brown sugar, cinnamon and banana liqueur, then flamed
>   in rum. Served over vanilla ice cream. Scandalously Delicious!

■ 3-Point Leading

>   Bananas Foster… A Brennan creation and now World Famous! Bananas
>   sautéed in butter, brown sugar, cinnamon and banana liqueur, then flamed
>   in rum. Served over vanilla ice cream. Scandalously Delicious!

■ 4-Point Leading

>   Bananas Foster… A Brennan creation and now World Famous! Bananas
>   sautéed in butter, brown sugar, cinnamon and banana liqueur, then flamed
>   in rum. Served over vanilla ice cream. Scandalously Delicious!

■ 5-Point Leading

>   Bananas Foster… A Brennan creation and now World Famous! Bananas
>   sautéed in butter, brown sugar, cinnamon and banana liqueur, then flamed
>   in rum. Served over vanilla ice cream. Scandalously Delicious!

FIGURE 8-3 Samples of Leading.

the background is dark, this is called **reversed type.** Avoid reversed type on the inside of a menu. Reverse type is acceptable on the cover of the menu however.

There are many variations of typefaces (see Figures 8-4, 8-5, and 8-6). These variations also include lowercase and uppercase letters. **Lowercase letters** are small letters, and **uppercase letters** are the capital or large letters. Lowercase letters should be used in descriptive copy on the menu, and uppercase letters should be used for headings or subheadings on the menu.

Menu planners also must decide whether or not to use the italic version of the typeface. The **italic** version of the typeface is angled or slanted and makes the menu more difficult to read. This form of type should be used only for headings or subheadings and to highlight items on the menu.

Color

The colors selected for the paper and type on a menu should match. A red background with yellow lettering, for instance, would clash horribly. On the other hand, pink paper with red type would blend well together. Professional printers or graphic artists can help the menu planner coordinate the colors of the paper and the type.

Balance

A menu is balanced when the number of menu offerings in the various categories are proportionately balanced. For example, if a menu has 12 appetizers, 2 soups, 4 salads, 20 entrées, and 8 desserts, the menu is considered to be well balanced. If there are a greater number of entrées than other items, this is not only acceptable but also recommended, because entrées are the focus of the menu and are usually the most expensive food items on the menu.

Variety

Variety is crucial to a good menu. Variety is important not only for the number of selections offered within a category but also for the way in which food items are prepared. For example, an appetizer category on a

A B C D E F G H I J K L M
N O P Q R S T U V W X Y Z
a b c d e f g h i j k l m
n o p q r s t u v w x y z
1 2 3 4 5 6 7 8 9 0 $
1 2 3 4 5 6 7 8 9 0 [& ( )

7 Point Size:

9 Point Size:

10 Point Size:

12 Point Size:

14 Point Size:

16 Point Size:

18 Point Size:

20 Point Size:

24 Point Size:

28 Point Size:

30 Point Size:

36 Point Size:

42 Point Size:

48 Point Size:

54 Point Size:

60 Point Size:

FIGURE 8-4 Cooper Black Typeface.

A B C D E F G H I J K L M

N O P Q R S T U V W X Y Z

a b c d e f g h i j k l m

n o p q r s t u v w x y z

1 2 3 4 5 6 7 8 9 0 $

- — ? & • / * ( ) " " # %

10 Point Size

12 Point Size:

14 Point Size:

16 Point Size:

18 Point Size:

20 Point Size:

24 Point Size:

28 Point Size:

30 Point Size:

36 Point Size:

42 Point Size:

48 Point Size:

54 Point Size:

60 Point Size:

72 Point Size:

FIGURE 8-5 London Script Typeface.

Eras Light
Eras Medium
Eras Bold
Eras Outline
Eras Contour
Fat Face
Fat Face Condensed
Fortune Bold
Franklin Gothic
Franklin Gothic Extra Cond
FRIEND
Friz Quadrata
Friz Quadrata Bold
Futura Black
Futura Bold
Futura Bold Italic
Futura Demibold
Futura Medium
Futura Medium Italic
GOLD RUSH
Gorilla
Grizzly
Grotesque No. 9

ACCENT
Advertisers Gothic
AKI LINES
Amer. Typewriter Bold
American Typewriter Bold Cond
Amer. Typewriter Medium
American Typewriter Med Cond
Arpad Light
Astur
Avant Garde Bold
Avant Garde Book
Avant Garde Med.
Avant Garde Bold Condensed
Avant Garde Medium Condensed
Bauhaus Medium
Bauhaus Heavy
Bauhaus Heavy Outline
BLACKLINE
Blippo Black
Bolt Bold
Bookman Bold
Bookman Bold Italic
Bookman Contour

MACHINE
MANDARIN
Manhattan
Microgramma Bold Extended
Microgramma Extended
MOORE COMPUTER
NEON
Newtext Book
Newtext Demi
Old English
Optima
Palace Script
Peignot Bold
Peignot Light
PIONEER
Playbill
PROFIL
Ronda
RUSTIC
SAPPHIRE
Serif Gothic Black
Serif Gothic Bold
Serif Gothic Ex. Bold

FIGURE 8-6 Samples of Various Typefaces.

menu that includes Clams Casino, Crab Cakes, Portobello Mushrooms, Carpaccio, and Cantaloupe and Berries offers a good variety. Entrées can be steamed, broiled, sautéed, poached, braised, boiled, fried, roasted, or simmered. Customers appreciate variety on a menu. Variety also reflects a chef's creativity.

Composition

The composition of menu item groupings is important in planning a menu. The menu planner must evaluate how well certain dishes go with particular entrées. Sweet potatoes, for example, are excellent with ham, just as popovers are good with roast beef. In general, when entrées have a lot of flavor, side dishes should have a less pronounced flavor. Beef Stroganoff might be served with peas or carrots, for example. On the other hand, if entrées that are less rich are served, side dishes should have more flavor. One example might be pairing an entrée of Baked Chicken with Zucchini Provençale (zucchini, tomatoes, bread crumbs, Parmesan cheese, garlic, and assorted spices).

Another way to address composition is through eye appeal. Colors of foods have tremendous eye appeal when they are used properly in the composition of menu items. A plate of Baked Haddock (white), steamed broccoli (green), and stewed tomatoes (ruby red), for example, would reflect good color and composition. Eye appeal enhances customer satisfaction.

Descriptive Copy

Descriptive copy offers an explanation of how an item is prepared and served. It is the descriptive copy that helps to sell an item on the menu. Entrées on a menu should have the most elaborate descriptive copy, because they are the most expensive items on the menu. One important rule the menu planner should remember when composing descriptive copy is to avoid the use of words that describe the killing process, such as *slaughtered* or *butchered*. In the United States, English should be used in descriptive copy in ethnic menus.

Descriptive copy that is used by all foodservice operations fits into one of three philosophies of profit management. The exclusive gourmet menu with a high check average uses a substantial amount of descriptive copy. This type of foodservice operation wants the customer to dine for a period of one-and-a-half or two hours. More descriptive copy on a menu gives customers more information about the items on the menu, and it also keeps customers in the restaurant longer by giving them more to read.

The second philosophy of profit management requires little or no descriptive copy on its menu. This type of operation uses a short, limited menu and looks for a rapid turnover rate, expecting customers to stay only 15 to 20 minutes. The food selections are limited and simply stated, along with the price, thus reducing the time needed for the customer to decide on what he or she wishes to order.

The third philosophy, the family-style foodservice operation, lists food items such as appetizers, desserts, and beverages, and gives descriptive copy for the soups, salads, and entrées. This type of operation wants its customers to eat and enjoy themselves for approximately 45 minutes to one hour.

Truth-in-Menu

Each and every item described on the menu must be completely accurate. Truth-in-menu laws exist in several states to deter deceptive advertising on the menu. Fines, court expenses, and negative publicity can result if a restaurant violates such laws. The National Restaurant Association published an "Accuracy in Menu" position paper in February 1977, in an effort to assist menu planners in preparing descriptions that accurately represent the items listed on a menu (see Appendix G).

Menu Labeling

In 1990, Congress passed menu labeling regulations under the Nutritional Labeling and Education Act (NLEA). Although they were initially designed for the packaged food industry to substantiate nutrient claims, the regulations were revised in May 1994 to include claims made on placards, posters, and signs in restaurants. By 1995, all restaurants had to comply with the menu labeling regulations. Beginning on May 2, 1997, the Food and Drug Administration (FDA) determined that all nutrient and health claims on menus had to be scientifically substantiated as well. All segments of the foodservice industry were required to adhere to these regulations, including caterers, delicatessens, take-out establishments, restaurants, and institutional foodservice operations.

Once a restaurant makes a nutrient or health claim regarding a menu item, it must substantiate that claim. A **nutrient claim** makes a statement about the presence of a particular nutrient in a menu item. Words such as *cholesterol-free, fresh, healthy, natural, low in fat, light,* and *reduced* are commonly used on menus. A **health claim** states that there is a relationship between a food item or meal and disease prevention, for example, fruits and vegetables in relation to cancer prevention.

The FDA recognizes recipes appearing in published cookbooks that have a nutritional analysis for each recipe, computer-generated databases, and menus endorsed by dietary or health professional organizations as acceptable sources of nutrient and health claims. Nutrient and health claims need not appear directly on the menu, but they must be made available to all patrons either through a brochure, pamphlet, recipe file, notebook, bulletin board, or poster. Menus that do not make nutrient or health claims need not adhere to these regulations.

Listing of Items

Items should be presented on the menu in the order in which they will be consumed. Most menus list appetizers, soups, salads, entrées and accompaniments, and then desserts, in that order. A French classical menu, on the other hand, would list the salads just before the desserts. The most profitable food items should be listed first and last in a particular category. The most popular and least profitable food items should be listed in the middle. When reading down a column of any list, a person usually will look at the first few items, skim the middle section, and then read the last few items before looking at the next column. The most popular items are likely to be ordered, regardless of their place on the menu.

The best location for the most profitable items is in the top half of quadrangle 2 on a single-fold menu (see Figure 8-7). When a customer opens a menu from right to left, the first page or quadrangles seen are

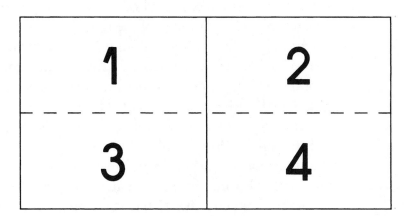

FIGURE 8-7 Diagram of a Single-Fold Menu.

2 and 4, or the second page. Having learned to read from left to write, customers will start reading at quadrangle 1 but will first actually see quadrangle 2.

Entrées conveniently fall into place on the right after the list of appetizers, soups, and salads on the left. High-profit entrées such as chicken and pasta should come first under the entrée headings, then lobster, sirloin, and veal.

Size of Menu

The menu should be large enough to merchandise the food items without them appearing crowded on the page. Too large a menu can be awkward to handle. The most popular menu size is 8 1/2 inches by 11 inches. Avoid type that is too small for customers to read. Most menus are made up of four pages. The cover forms pages 1 and 4, and the list of menu items inside makes up pages 2 and 3.

Cover Design

The front and back covers provide an opportunity for tremendous merchandising power. The cover of a menu should reflect the decor and the theme of the operation. A specialty restaurant, for example, that features broiled steaks and that uses red tablecloths and black napkins might want a red menu cover with black print.

The front cover should carry the name of the restaurant and a recognizable symbol or logo of the restaurant. The logo of a seafood restaurant called "The White Cap" might be an anchor or an embossed wave. The back cover of the menu might list the address and phone number of the restaurant or any other information, such as that credit cards are accepted at the establishment. Hours of operation, restaurant history, and banquet or take-out service might also appear on the back cover. Surprisingly enough, only 50 percent of restaurants use the back covers of their menus for merchandising purposes.

It is also important to remember that the menu cover should be durable, water-resistant, and stain-resistant, unless the menu changes daily and is disposable.

Review Questions

1. What factors should be taken into consideration when a menu planner is selecting paper for a menu?

2. How are uppercase and lowercase type used on a menu?

3. What is "reverse type"?

4. How is type measured?

5. What is "leading"?

6. What is "balance"?

7. How can variety be added to a menu?

8. What are two aspects of composition?

9. In what order should items be listed on a menu?

10. Which items might be listed on the back cover of a menu?

Additional Reading

Albin G. Seaborg, *Menu Design Merchandising and Marketing,* 4th ed. (New York: John Wiley & Sons, 1991).

Chapter 9

Sales History

*I*n this chapter, we will discuss the use of sales history and the importance of the computerized goal value program. In order to plan your future, it is wise to take a look at your past.

Objectives

1. To explain the importance of a sales history report
2. To teach the student how to complete a sales history report
3. To demonstrate how to solve a goal-value analysis problem

Sales History Background

The **sales history,** also known as a **scatter sheet mix,** is a daily record of the menu items that have been sold. The sales history contains any information that will help to explain the sales volume for a particular day. The following list demonstrates the numerous uses of this document:

- To forecast
- To keep a daily record of which food items were sold
- To keep a daily record of how many menu items were sold
- To predict sales volume
- To record information that will aid management in forecasting accurately
- To aid management in predicting a sales analysis
- To project the annual budget
- To aid management in determining the dollar amount that customers are willing to pay

The purpose of a sales history is to help management accurately forecast the foodservice operation's needs. It is a difficult task for management to forecast the number of customers that it thinks will be dining at its foodservice operation in the future and the amount of supplies that it will need to accomodate those customers. If management purchases too many supplies, then profits are lost; if it does not purchase enough supplies, customers will be dissatisfied. Keeping a daily record of the actual menu items that have been sold and the number of items that have been sold helps management to forecast more accurately.

The factor that makes a sales history worthwhile is the theory that history repeats itself. In most cases, foodservice management teams would agree that customer sales volumes are predictable to a certain degree of accuracy. For example, a seasonal foodservice operation in the New England area might open on weekends plus one or two days during the week out of season.

After Memorial Day, sales volume slowly starts to increase week by week, because 90 percent of colleges have ended their academic year. In June, sales volume continues to grow as the elementary and secondary school year ends. During July, sales volume increases substantially, because this is when many people begin to take their vacations. In August and September, foodservice operations reach their peak season sales volume. August is a favorite month for family vacations, because the children are out of school and the weather is at its warmest. In September, once Labor Day arrives, the volume of families traveling is drastically reduced, because children are back in school. However, the foodservice operation does not yet close for the season. There are still a considerable number of people who prefer to vacation after Labor Day in order to avoid the extreme summer temperatures and crowds. After September, the weekly sales volume decreases enough for a seasonal operation to close its doors.

Keeping a sales history on the volume of menu items sold will help management in purchasing the correct amount of supplies. By analyzing the sales volume of the past, it is possible to predict the sales volume of the future. When analyzing the sales history, you should compare the history of the same time periods; that is, compare Monday's business with Monday's business. Do not compare Monday's business with that of another business day. Each day has its own unique characteristics. For example, Monday is usually the slowest day of the week. On Mondays, customers have little disposable income left over from the weekend. Also, most people are recuperating from weekend activities and are likely to relax at home when they return from work. In constrast, Saturday is the busiest day of the week, because people have disposable income to spend and they are off from work.

It is also important to compare the same meal periods (i.e., breakfast, lunch, dinner) on the same day of the week. Breakfast, lunch, and dinner have their own unique characteristics. Breakfast attracts a different type of customer, check average, and turnover rate than lunch and dinner. In actuality, these meals are three different types of businesses operating under one roof.

In order to forecast the number of customers for each meal period accurately, it is necessary for you to have pertinent information that influences sales on that particular day. Examples of such information are:

- Day of the week
- Date
- Weather
- Time of day
- Meal period
- Special events within the community that will produce more sales, such as concerts, conventions, meetings, and bus tours
- Employees who are absent from work that day

It is a difficult task to be 100 percent accurate in forecasting each day's needs and to always achieve maximum profit for that day. With experience and a knowledge of the type of customers that frequent your foodservice operation, as well as of the surrounding community, forecasting can be very accurate and an exciting tool.

Benefits of the Scatter Sheet

At the end of each meal period, the food items that are sold must be recorded onto the sales history ledger. This information is usually taken from the register slip. Once this information has been recorded, the management team must analyze the results. This analysis should be done on a daily, weekly, and monthly basis. The management team should be looking for menu items that are not selling and whether or not the sales are in line with the annual sales projection.

If a restaurant is losing sales, the sales history record can be helpful in determining the problem. Most restaurants lose sales because customers do not like the approach that the restaurant is taking in one or more of the following areas:

- Sanitation
- Quality of the food

- Quality of the service
- Prices
- Atmosphere
- Location of the restaurant

The sales history helps to determine which menu items are selling and which ones are not. (It is up to management to determine why the food items are not selling and to correct the problem.) It could be that prices are too high, portions are too small or too large, the food presentation is not attractive, or any of several other possibilities. Once management knows the reason behind the poor sales of an item, it should promote the food item or take the item off the menu.

A scatter sheet is used by management when it is making its annual budgetary projection. Management needs to maintain a daily sales record of the amount of money made each day. Weekly profits should be compared with annual profits and expense projections. If sales drop for three consecutive weeks, it is highly unlikely that the sales loss will be regained. Management cannot afford to wait until the beginning of the fourth quarter to check its profits and expense projections. By then, it is too late to recover losses that have occurred earlier in the year.

It is helpful to determine the cost of foods on a menu and to eliminate items that are not selling. For example, when a restaurant sells 100 portions of prime rib at $8.95 per portion, this generates $895. If management increases the price of the prime rib to $11.95, and the number of portions sold decreases to 60 portions, there is a yield of only $717.00, reducing profit by $178. If management reduces the price to $10.95, and the number of portions sold increases to 90, the restaurant is now making $90.50 more in profit and management has established the price that the market is willing to pay for the prime rib. The sales history keeps a record of how the prime rib is selling at those different price levels.

How a Scatter Sheet Works

The scatter sheet is composed of several elements (see Figure 9-1). Column 1 includes the week ending date, the menu item listings, the remarks area, and the meal period area. Column 2 includes the name of the restaurant and space for the weather and the days of the week. To

	Column 1		Column 2					Col. 3	Col. 4	Col. 5	Col. 6	Col. 7
	MENU SCATTER SHEET: BRIAN'S RESTAURANT Week Ending: 6/14/85 Weather: clear, 70°F							Weekly No. Sold	Selling Price	Item Sales	Total Weekly Sales	% Contribution to Sales
				TALLY								
Menu Item	Mon	Tue	Wed	Thu	Fri	Sat	Sun					
N.E. Chowder	5	8	10	12	20	30	20	105	$ 0.95	$ 99.75	$16093.65	0.00619
French Onion	7	7	12	11	25	23	29	114	1.25	142.50		0.00885
Tossed Salad	30	40	50	60	70	65	66	381	0.85	323.85		0.02012
Greek Salad	3	4	2	0	1	3	1	14	0.95	13.30		0.00082
Broiled Lobster	15	20	30	31	32	35	50	213	14.95	3184.35		0.19786
Baked Stuff Lobster	16	35	32	40	45	65	55	288	16.95	4881.60		0.30332
Fried Clams	20	25	33	16	10	70	65	239	8.95	2139.05		0.13291
Broiled Scallops	10	15	20	25	30	35	40	175	9.95	1741.25		0.10819
Sirloin Steak	8	10	1.5	7	20	25	45	130	10.50	1365.00		0.08481
Tenderloin Strip	19	18	17	12	11	13	15	105	12.50	1312.50		0.08155
Half Roast Duck	7	6	4	3	2	0	8	30	11.50	345.00		0.02143
Baked Potato	35	38	40	55	85	90	110	453	0.50	226.50		0.01407
Mashed Potato	20	19	35	20	15	12	20	141	0.50	70.50		0.00438
Peas	15	20	22	23	28	32	45	185	0.35	64.75		0.00402
Corn	20	25	31	38	39	41	46	240	0.35	84.00		0.00521
Carrots	35	39	40	41	42	43	45	285	0.35	99.75		0.00619
											$16093.65	
Etc.												
Etc.												
Remarks:												
Meal Period: Dinner 6:00–10:00 P.M.												

FIGURE 9-1 Sales History Form: Scatter Sheet.

find out how much of a particular item has been sold, do one of the following:

1. Review the meal checks and count the times that a particular item was sold.

2. Program the cash register to keep a tally of each item on the menu so that you can take a reading from the register tape.

Column 3 shows the weekly total of the individual menu items that were sold. Column 4 shows the selling price of the individual item. Column 5 shows the items' sales, which is calculated by multiplying column 3 by column 4. Column 6 shows the total of weekly sales, calculated by adding the totals of the individual items in column 5. Column 7 shows the percentage contribution to sales, indicating the contributing percentage of sales of the individual menu item to the total weekly sales of all of the items on the menu. This amount is calculated by dividing column 5 by column 6.

The Production Sheet

A **production sheet** is a schedule that gives the following information to employees:

- Who will be doing what task
- When they will be doing the task
- Where they will be doing the task
- What equipment they will need
- The quantity of a product they will need

The sales history form is extremely helpful in assisting the chef in determining the quantity of food that the cooks will need to prepare for production. The chef should refer to the sales history when he or she is making out the production sheet in order to see what was sold during the same time frame the week before. By reviewing the sales history, the chef will know how much to prepare.

Goal-Value Analysis

As we have seen, sales history is one way in which you can analyze menu items. Another alternative to menu analysis is goal-value analysis. **Goal-value analysis** is a simple, comprehensive technique that was developed by David K. Hayes and Lynn Huffman. Goal-value analysis compares the profit contribution of an individual menu item with the average profit performance of the total business.

The business information that is necessary to do a typical goal-value analysis is presented in Table 9-1, including total sales in dollars, food cost percentage, labor cost percentage, other controllable cost percentage, and profit percentage (see also Table 9-2).

Table 9-1   INFORMATION NECESSARY FOR A GOAL-VALUE ANALYSIS

Income Statement Information for a Hypothetical Restaurant

Sales for the week	$24,780.00 = 100%
Food cost %	31.4% = Controllable cost = $7,780.92
Labor cost %	34.1% = Controllable cost = $8,449.98
Other controllable cost % (Food, labor, and overhead)	15.6% = Controllable cost = $3,865.68
Uncontrollable cost % (Interest, depreciation, insurance, licenses, real estate taxes, and income taxes)	11.1% = $2,750.58
Profit %	7.8% = $1,932.84

Note: Controllable cost % = food cost % from recipes + labor cost % + other controllable cost %. Total sales = 100% = food cost % + labor cost % + other controllable cost % + uncontrollable cost % + profit %

Menu Item	Food Cost % (from costed recipes)	% Contribution to Sales (from point of sales cash register)	Selling Price (from menu)	Number Sold
Fried Squid	33.7	3.0	$2.00	372
Pizza	42.1	37.0	$6.85	1,338
Eggplant	31.2	7.0	$0.75	2,313
Pepsi	18.6	26.0	$0.75	8,590
Amaretto Cheese cake	28.2	27.0	$3.45	1,939

Note: A point of sales cash register is an electronic cash register that can determine the contribution to sales of a food and beverage item as the sale occurs.

Number sold (# sold) = sales · contribution to sales/selling price. For example, number of fried squid sold = (24,780 × 3%)/$2.00 = 372.

$\mathcal{T}able$ 9-2 Goal-Value Analysis Worksheet

Goal Value (overall standard) =

(1 − FC% <u>0.686</u>) × (ANS <u>2910</u>) × (ASP <u>1.70</u>) × [1 − (LC% <u>0.341</u> + OCC% <u>0.156</u> + FC% <u>0.314</u>)] =
   0.189

<u>641.398</u>

Menu Item Value (use all percentages in decimal form)

Menu Item	Food Cost %	Contrib. Cost %	Number Sold	×	Selling Price	×	1 − FC%	×	1 − CC%	=	Value
Fried Squid	0.337	0.834	372	×	2.00	×	0.663	×	0.166	=	81.883
Pizza	0.421	0.918	1338	×	6.85	×	0.579	×	0.082	=	435.150
Eggplant	0.312	0.809	2313	×	0.75	×	0.688	×	0.191	=	227.960
Pepsi	0.186	0.683	8590	×	0.75	×	0.814	×	0.317	=	1662.409
Amaretto Cheesecake	0.282	0.779	1939	×	3.45	×	0.718	×	0.221	=	1061.484

Total number sold	= 14,552
Average number sold	= 14,552/5 (number of menu items sold)
Average selling price	= 24,780.00 (sales)/14,552 (total number sold)
Number sold	= Sales × % contribution to sales/selling price
Controllable cost %	= Food cost % from recipes + labor cost % + other controllable cost %
Value	= Number sold × selling price × (1 − food cost %) × (1 − controllable cost %)

Note: Number sold contributes a popularity factor. *Selling price* contributes a ticket size factor. 1 − *food cost* % contributes a food cost factor. 1 − *controllable cost* contributes a profit factor.

The goal value overall (overall standard) is compared to the value of the menu item. If the value is higher than the goal value (overall standard), the menu item is a winner. However, if the value is lower than the goal value (overall standard), the menu item is a loser. Sometimes, though, a low-value item should not be taken off the menu, because it may be a favorite of loyal customers, who, in turn, will bring in other customers. Therefore, it is important to remember that goal-value analysis is merely a tool to aid foodservice professionals in analyzing menu items, and it needs to be considered a part of the process of carefully analyzing costs.

Goal-value analysis not only demonstrates the profitability of existing menu items but also can be used for analyzing menu items before they are placed on a menu. The following formula shows the minimum sales volume that is necessary for a new menu item to generate a profit.

$$\frac{\text{Goal value (Overall standard)}}{\text{Actual Food cost \% × Actual selling price × Food cost}}$$

$$= \text{Sales volume goal}$$

Here is an example, for a new menu item—Antipasto:

Food cost % = 32.7%

Selling price = $2.50

Labor cost % = 34.1%

Other controllable costs % = 15.6%

$$\frac{641.398}{0.683 \times 2.50 \times 0.186} = \text{Sales volume goal}$$
$$2,016.98 = \text{Sales volume goal}$$

This restaurant must have a sales volume goal of 2,017 in order to make antipasto a profitable item on the menu.

 *Review Questions*

1. Why can't a manager compare Monday's sales with Tuesday's sales?

2. Which day of the week is usually the slowest for most foodservice operations?

3. What is meant by the term "disposable income"?

4. Define "sales history".

5. In what two areas is the sales history analysis useful to management?

6. Define goal-value analysis.

 *Additional Readings*

David K. Hayes and Lynn Huffman, Menu Analysis: A Better Way, *The Cornell HRA Quarterly*, February 1985.

Paul R. Dittmer and Gerald G. Griffin, *Principles of Food, Beverage and Labor Cost Controls*, 6th edition. (New York: John Wiley & Sons, 1999).

Lendal H. Kotschevar and Marcel R. Escoffier, *Management by Menu*, (Chicago, IL: Educational Foundation of the National Restaurant Association, 1994).

Paul J. McVety, Sue Marshall, and Bradley J. Ware, *The Menu and the Cycle of Cost Control*. (Dubuque, IA: Kendall/Hunt Publisher, 1997).

Software Programs Available

These software packages offer sales analysis information:

ExecuChef Software: visit www.execuchef.com

Tracrite and Optimum Control Restaurant Management Software: visit www.tracrite.net

Johnson Technologies, Inc.: visit www.johnsontech.com

Chapter 10

Merchandising the Menu

*F*or a menu to be successful, it is not enough that it be accurately costed. A menu also must be properly presented. Proper presentation is the key to producing a well-merchandised menu. If a menu planner does not appropriately list liquors or wines, or fails to describe popular items effectively, this may have a devastating effect on sales. The major function of a menu is to sell menu items, but this can only occur when careful marketing and merchandising take place. This chapter examines the importance of marketing and merchandising when you are planning a menu.

 ## Objectives

1. To provide an explanation of how items can be effectively and appropriately merchandised on a menu
2. To analyze and evaluate the merchandising power of an actual menu

Merchandising is the presentation of a product to the appropriate market at the right time in an organized and attractive display. A well-merchandised menu is a successful menu. Consideration of the following areas is extremely important when you are merchandising a menu:

the listing of additional pertinent information, the listing of liquors, wines, appetizers, salads, low-calorie items, steaks, seafood, sandwiches, desserts, take-out service, and specials.

Displaying Additional Information on the Menu

Additional information on a menu is practical information that is provided to customers to better serve and accommodate them. Additional information might include a list of credit cards accepted by the establishment, the hours of operation, the address and phone number of the restaurant, catering information, take-out service, banquet accommodations, gift shop information, local tourist attractions, information about other locations if the property is part of a chain, and possibly a history of the property itself. Many establishments do not include additional information on their menus, yet the back cover of a menu does provide a great opportunity for valuable merchandising power.

Listing Liquors

In most restaurants, management does not typically list liquors on the menu. It is often the job of the waitstaff person to take the drink order without a customer seeing a list. Mentioning liquor or wine on the menu often increases sales, even if there is also a separate beverage menu.

A separate liquor list or wine list tends to call attention to the selections available. A liquor list on the back cover of the menu is less effective for merchandising because it may be overlooked.

When you are listing liquors, give the brand name. For example, under vodka, you might give the recognizable brand name Smirnoff. It is also important to list liquors in the order in which they are consumed at mealtime. Before-dinner drinks consist of scotches, whiskeys, bourbons, gins, vodkas, and rums. Beers may come next, followed by wines (red, white, and champagnes), with brandies and liqueurs listed last. If you do not have a separate after-dinner drink menu, list these drinks after desserts on a separate page.

Wine Lists

A large wine selection should be presented on a separate wine list. A smaller wine selection can be included on the main menu, paired with entrées, or it may appear on the liquor menu.

It is always good merchandising to give descriptive copy with wines. Who could resist a Chablis (Drouhin) from the burgundy class made from Chardonnay grapes, very dry, with a rich body?

Appetizers

Appetizers should be listed before soups on the menu. Good copy that is easy to read will aid in selling appetizers. Six to ten appetizers on an average size à la carte menu provide good balance. Variety is important. The number of appetizer offerings should increase as the number of entrées increases.

Salads

Salads should be listed after the appetizers and the soups. Salads, like appetizers, should be set in readable type and should be given appropriate descriptive copy. A chef's salad might be described as "a generous portion of romaine, iceberg, and Bibb lettuce, topped with Danish ham, Genoa salami, smoked turkey, sliced tomatoes, cucumbers, green peppers, and sliced hard-boiled eggs, with a side of the house's own Thousand Island dressing. A complete meal in itself."

A description of the salad dressing itself can be important on the menu. An example might be: "a Thousand Island dressing made with rich mayonnaise, ketchup, Worcestershire sauce, relish, assorted spices, and just a touch of Tabasco sauce. A great dressing for any salad."

Low-Calorie Items

Today, people are much more aware about what they eat and whether or not what they eat is nutritionally sound. Many customers eat low-calorie items, the most popular of which are salads. A low-calorie fruit salad might be listed under salads, listing the assortment of fruits in the descriptive copy.

Steaks

Steaks require descriptive copy for better merchandising on a menu. There are many factors for you to consider when you are describing steaks, for example, the cut of the steak, the thickness, size, portion, and the manner in which it is prepared. Effective descriptive copy for a steak might read: "A 12 oz cut of filet broiled to perfection and topped with a creamy Hollandaise sauce with assorted spices."

Information that is provided in order to assist patrons in ordering a steak rare, medium rare, medium, or well done is also valuable. Steaks are one of the most expensive items on a menu and should be described well and placed on the right-hand side of the menu.

Seafood

Seafood, like steak, should be listed in large, easy-to-read type and should have adequate descriptive copy. Information concerning where the seafood comes from and how it is prepared and served is needed. An example of descriptive copy for a seafood selection might read: "Scrod Bella Vista—a generous portion of baked scrod, topped with sliced onions, green peppers, and tomatoes, surrounded by a rich tomato sauce."

Sandwiches

Sandwiches also should have good descriptive copy in easy-to-read type. If sandwiches are a specialty item, they should be listed before the entrées. However, it is common practice to list only the most popular and profitable sandwiches after the entrées. Hot sandwiches on the menu can be given more extensive descriptive copy than cold sandwiches, if they are more profitable items.

Desserts

Desserts can be listed in two ways. The first method is to clearly list desserts with descriptive copy after entrées on the menu. The second method is to have a separate dessert menu that may also include after-dinner drinks and specialty coffees and teas. The separate dessert menu offers a greater amount of space in which to describe dessert items elaborately, drawing greater attention to those items.

Take-Out Service

Take-out service requires proper merchandising. The best way to merchandise take-out service is to prepare a separate take-out menu. When you are listing take-out information, give proper descriptive copy in readable type, prices, portions, and packaging. Include a phone number, if delivery service is available. Advertising for take-out service can be placed on the back cover of the in-house menu as well.

Specials

There can be two types of specials on a menu. The first type is the one for which the restaurant might be well known. The second type might be the type that generates a high profit. To encourage customers to try the specials, use pictures on the menu, as many specialty establishments do, or place the specials inside a box or a graphic panel to attract attention.

Evaluating the Sales Menu

The special occasion menu that follows will be evaluated for print, balance, variety, composition, descriptive copy, listing of items, and color.

Printing

The print is clear and easy to read. The headings are printed in uppercase letters, and the descriptive copy is printed in lowercase roman typeface.

Balance

The balance on this menu is poor because of the limited choices in the selection of entrées and vegetables. There should be a minimum of two vegetable choices and two potato choices. The entrées should include one other selection, such as Baked Ham with Raisin Sauce.

Variety

The variety offered on a special occasion menu is usually limited, because certain foods are traditional for that occasion, as seen on this Thanksgiving menu. Besides the limited selection of vegetables and entrées, the variety of the other food categories is good.

Composition

The eye appeal and aesthetic value of the menu items are fairly good. To present a more colorful plate, a green vegetable such as broccoli or peas is recommended.

Descriptive Copy

The descriptive copy is written in an interesting and appetizing fashion. The length of the copy for each item is not too long or overly detailed. The food items are clearly and precisely described.

Listing of Items

The food categories are listed in the proper serving sequence of appetizer, soups, salads, entrées, vegetables, desserts, and beverages. The prix fixe menu includes the entire meal at a set price.

Color

The colors used on the menu should include earth tones, such as browns, oranges, yellows, and greens. The graphics on the menu relate to the occasion being celebrated and include turkeys, pies, pumpkins, and other autumnal specialties.

The Inn at Kearsarge

GREAT BEGINNINGS

Stuffed Mushroom Caps

Mushrooms stuffed with crabmeat, breadcrumbs, sautéed onions, green peppers, pimentos and just the right amount of sherry and spices.

Apple Cider

This cider comes piping hot with a cinnamon stick to add a special taste.

SOUPS

French Onion Soup

Our soup is simmered slowly and served in a crock dripping with swiss cheese and topped with croutons.

Potato and Leek Soup

This soup is loaded with potatoes and leeks in a rich creamy base.

SALADS

Fruit Salad

An assortment of oranges, apples, grapefruit, strawberries and blueberries capped with lime sherbert and served in a chilled cocktail glass.

Garden Salad

This salad is brimming with romaine, iceberg, boston bibb, cherry tomatoes, cucumbers, radishes, carrots, mushrooms, and chopped eggs. Topped with our own creamy Italian or Thousand Island Dressing.

FIGURE 10-1 Special Occasion Menu. (Prepared by the Authors)

THE MAIN COURSE

Roast Turkey and Dressing

Your choice of light or dark meat with our chestnut stuffing and, of course, our homemade cranberry sauce.

Broiled Sirloin Steak with Bordelaise Sauce

Our steak is broiled to perfection and covered with a rich brown sauce with sautéed mushrooms.

FROM THE GARDEN

Acorn Squash

We cook this squash slowly and sprinkle it with brown sugar, butter, cinnamon and a hint of nutmeg.

Sweet Potatoes

This dish is an all-time favorite. We combine pineapple, marshmallows, sweet potatoes and top this side dish with brown sugar and butter.

DESSERTS

Pumpkin Pie

A rich dessert, baked in a whole wheat crust and topped with whipped cream.

Grapenut Pudding

A smooth blend of grapenuts, apples, molasses, brown sugar, with whipped cream. This dessert is a great way to finish any holiday feast.

BEVERAGES

Coffee, tea or milk.

ADULTS — $16.25   CHILDREN — $9.25

(Tax and gratuity included.)

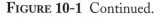

FIGURE 10-1 Continued.

Review Questions

1. Name five pieces of information that might be listed on the back cover of a menu.

2. Identify some important principles when you are listing liquors.

3. How are wine selections presented?

4. Why is it important to offer low-calorie items on a menu?

5. What are some descriptive words used on a menu to describe steaks?

6. List key words used to describe seafood.

7. What are two important factors that affect the listing of sandwiches on a menu?

8. List two ways in which desserts might be listed.

9. How can a menu planner highlight specials on a menu?

10. What is the best way to market take-out service?

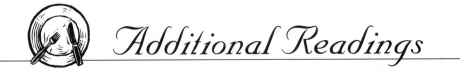

Additional Readings

Lendal H. Kotschevar and Marcel R. Escoffier, *Management by Menu*, 3rd ed. (Chicago, IL: The Educational Foundation of the National Restaurant Association, 1994).

Albin G. Seaborg, *Menu Design Merchandising and Marketing*, 4th ed. (New York: John Wiley & Sons, 1991).

Chapter 11

Foodservice Equipment Analysis

*E*very foodservice operator needs to purchase equipment in order to produce the food products on the menu. This chapter establishes guidelines for selecting equipment and explains how to justify the equipment that the foodservice operator needs to buy.

 *Objectives*

1. To show the student how to purchase foodservice equipment without overpurchasing

2. To show the student how to complete a foodservice equipment analysis and establish a listing of foodservice equipment that indicates the capacity of the equipment

3. To identify ten guidelines that should be used when purchasing equipment

Guidelines for Selecting Equipment

It is essential for any foodservice operator who wants to stay within a budget to be knowledgeable about the types and the volume of equipment to be purchased. The following are guidelines to purchasing equipment.

Justify the Purchase of the Equipment. If You Do Not Need It, Don't Buy It!

A lot of equipment is sold each year to foodservice operators who find that, after the sale, they have little or no use for it. How does one justify the purchase of equipment? Foodservice operators need to complete a foodservice equipment analysis. The purpose of the foodservice equipment analysis is to establish the type of equipment and the volume of equipment needed to produce the food products on the menu. Many foodservice operators rely totally on the sales representative to establish the type of equipment needed to produce the items on the menu. This dependence is harmful, because the sales representative does not have a knowledge of the entire foodservice operation. Most foodservice equipment sales representatives do not inflate the type and number of pieces of equipment that are needed. They make recommendations on what to buy based on the needs and desires of the foodservice operators. Always remember, however, that it is the sales representative's job to sell equipment and it is the foodservice operator's job to know what equipment to purchase.

Know When to Purchase New Equipment

When do you need to purchase new equipment? Purchase new equipment if the customer is going to be viewing the equipment. Factors that will influence this decision are the foodservice operation's budget and the image that it wants to portray. New equipment is primarily used in the front of the foodservice operation.

Consider purchasing used equipment. The primary advantage of purchasing used equipment is to save money. The National Restaurant Association reports that 80 percent of first-time foodservice operators in a given year fail due in part to the high cost of purchasing new equipment. The life span of a major piece of equipment, such as a broiler, fryer, or oven, is ten years. Purchasing used equipment that has been liquidated will save the buyer 30–50 percent of the sticker price of a new piece of equipment. One disadvantage of purchasing used equipment is that the equipment cannot be 100 percent depreciated by the second operator, if at all. Another is that the second owner may lose the benefits of the dealership guarantee or the manufacturer's warranty and will not know how well the liquidated equipment has been maintained.

The best place to purchase used equipment is at a liquidation auction. To be successful at purchasing liquidated equipment, the foodservice operator must not be in a rush to furnish the operation. It takes time, energy, money, patience, and knowledge about the needed equipment. The foodservice operator needs to contact the nearest auction house or to look in the newspaper to find out when an auction will be held.

It is important to preview the equipment in order to see if it does operate, and, if there is damage, to see whether it is repairable. Another important factor is to establish the amount of money you are willing to pay for each piece of equipment before the auction starts. You do not want to go over your budget during the bidding process. During the preview time, find out about the procedures that the auction house uses. Most auction houses require that the equipment be moved from the hall immediately after the auction. Also inquire about the types of payments that the auction house accepts. Personal checks and credit cards require a reference check, so most auction houses require that you establish this before the auction begins.

Banks are another source for locating foodservice equipment sales. Banks will hold auctions on the site of the foodservice operation on which they are foreclosing. Banks are the first to know if the foodservice operations themselves will be auctioned.

Learn about Renting versus Leasing Foodservice Equipment

The term *leasing* means renting with an option to purchase the equipment. When you are renting equipment, there is no option to purchase the equipment. The main reasons for renting and/or leasing equipment are as follows:

- If something goes wrong with the equipment, the foodservice operator does not have to pay for the service charge.
- If the equipment breaks while in operation, the foodservice operator does not have to pay for the spare parts.
- When a foodservice operation leases equipment, the operating capital that is needed to open the foodservice operation is less. More money is needed to purchase equipment than to rent or lease equipment.
- Eighty percent of people going into the foodservice business fail during the first year. If this happens, it is better not to own all of your equipment, because you will not be able to retain the total value or return on your investment. When you are leasing or renting equipment, the title of ownership is not owned by you; therefore, your loss is not as great.

Consider the Design of the Equipment

Always purchase equipment that will portray the image that you have selected. Purchase new equipment for places that the customer will see, and buy equipment that is operationally sound but may not be the best looking for other areas.

Purchase Equipment That Is Automated

Time is money! Purchase equipment that will allow you and your staff to save on the amount of time that it takes to do a task. Any automatic device, such as a timer on a fryolator, will allow the fry cook to cook the product and do another job at the same time.

Select Equipment That Is Self-cleaning or Easily Cleaned

Equipment that will clean itself is a miracle in disguise. A ventilation and exhaust hood system that has steam lines within the ducts and has an automatic timing device is an excellent example. The steam lines will release steam into the ducts (passageways of air to travel) at a set time to clean off the built-up grease. A self-cleaning piece of equipment will save energy and time. Easy-to-clean equipment, such as stainless steel tables, countertops, and shelves are an asset.

Select Equipment That Can Be Sanitized

Purchase equipment that has been certified to withstand the harsh chemicals that it takes to sanitize the equipment. The National Sanitation Foundation (NSF) is an organization that will test equipment to certify that the finish material on the equipment will withstand the reaction of the abrasive chemicals during the cleaning process. The Board of Health also looks at equipment to see that it can be taken apart easily so that it can be cleaned and sanitized. Look for NSF labels on the equipment.

Know about Guarantee versus Warranty

A warranty and a guarantee both protect your investment for a certain period of time. A **warranty** is issued by the manufacturer. It covers a time period of typically five years and protects the major "heart" component(s) of the equipment. A compressor or a walk-in freezer or cooler is an excellent example of a piece of equipment that usually comes with a warranty. If the compressor fails to operate under normal conditions, the warranty will allow the owner to have it serviced or replaced without charge. A **guarantee** is issued through the dealership where the equipment is purchased. It covers a time period of 30 days to two years, depending on the type of equipment. It protects small parts of a piece of equipment. For example, if the door handle to a walk-in freezer or cooler falls off, due to normal use, the owner can have it serviced without being charged.

Guarantees and warranties vary greatly from manufacturer to manufacture, so read them carefully. Make a copy of them, and file them separately from the originals.

Know about Selecting Standard Equipment and Building Your Own Specialized Equipment

Select standard equipment whenever possible. **Standard equipment** is equipment that has set a standard in the foodservice industry. It is equipment that comes from a company with a good reputation. Standard equipment is readily available and does not cost a lot of money to replace. Specialized equipment is designed and built to the foodservice operator's specifications. The equipment is designed to do a particular task in a foodservice operation. The advantages of standard equipment are:

- The availability of the equipment is greater.
- The price is less expensive.
- Spare parts are available at lower prices.
- Most foodservice equipment dealers carry the equipment.
- The service history has proven that the equipment is durable and has good production capabilities.
- A warranty and/or guarantee are available and most likely are for a longer period of time than those for specialized equipment.

One disadvantage of standard equipment is that sometimes the equipment cannot do the production task that you want it to do. Specialized equipment will cost more money to obtain and repair, but it is sometimes purchased because it is the only way to accomplish a certain task.

Check the Reputation of the Sales Dealership and Manufacturer

Research the reputation of the person or business from which you will be purchasing your equipment. You will be spending thousands of dollars on your equipment. Call the local Better Business Bureau, talk to former customers, and get references from persons or businesses to find out who they recommend. Talk with chefs, managers, and sales representatives to find out who they recommend as well.

Foodservice Equipment Analysis

To save money when you are purchasing equipment, develop a list of equipment that is essential for producing the menu. It is not wise to shop for equipment without first establishing your needs. Most people who do shop without a list end up spending more money on equipment than is necessary.

The purpose of a foodservice equipment analysis (see Figure 11-1) is to establish the type of equipment needed to produce a menu and to establish the volume or capacity of the equipment needed. The first step is to establish a menu. The second step is to calculate the number of portions to be prepared. This number is based on the foodservice operation's capacity times the turnover rate, plus a 10 percent growth rate. For example, a 100-seat foodservice operation times a three turnover rate per peak period hour (three hours) equals 300 customers. Add a 10 percent growth rate to plan for the future capacity of the equipment, thus allowing for 330 customers to be served during the peak period.

$$\begin{aligned}
\text{Portions to be prepared} &= [(\text{operation's capacity} \times \text{turnover rate}) \\
&\quad + 10\% \text{ growth rate}] \\
&= [(100 \times 3) + 10\%] \\
&= 300 + 30 \\
&= 330
\end{aligned}$$

A **peak period** is a period of time during which the foodservice operation will be very busy. The peak period for breakfast is usually three hours, between 6:00 A.M. and 9:00 A.M.; for lunch, it is between 11:00 A.M. and 2:00 P.M.; and for dinner, it is between 6:00 P.M. and 9:00 P.M. Peak periods will vary from operation to operation. The peak period in our example is from 6:00 P.M. to 9:00 P.M. on a Saturday night.

It is very important to forecast accurately the number of customers being served on a busy night or peak period. When a chef does not forecast accurately, food cost due to overproduction or underproduction will be high, which generates lower profits. Once you have established the total customer count, you must forecast how many portions of a menu product will be sold. For example, how many customers out of 330 will

FOODSERVICE EQUIPMENT ANALYSIS SHEET

Meal <u>Dinner</u>
Day <u>Saturday</u>
Peak Period <u>6:00 P.M. to 9:00 P.M.</u>

Meal Item	Portion to Prepare	Weight or Volume per Portion	Total Amount Produced	Items per Hour	Usage Time Range	EQUIPMENT: Including Size and Number			
						Preparation	Production	Holding	Service
Sirloin Steak	120	16 ozs	120 lbs	40	5-9 P.M.	walk-in cooler table reach-in cooler	broiler	reach-in cooler	

FIGURE 11-1 Foodservice Equipment Analysis Sheet.

purchase the sirloin steak entrée? A few factors that will influence your forecasted number are:

- Total number of steaks offered
- Popularity of the food product
- Price of the food product
- Amount of advertising or marketing done on the food product
- Quality of flavor (taste)
- Appearance
- Effort that the service staff is willing to make to sell the food product
- Rarity of the food product
- Order in which the menu items are listed
- Placement of the item on the menu
- Amount of time it takes to produce the food product

In our example (Figure 11-1), we will sell 120 portions during the peak period only. Once you have forecasted the number of portions that must be prepared, each portion is given a weight in ounces or pounds or a volume measurement, such as cups, pints, quarts, or gallons. The portion size of the sirloin steak is 16 ounces. (1 pound). To find the total amount produced, multiply the number of portions that must be prepared times the portion size:

$$120 \times 16 \text{ oz} = 1,920 \text{ oz } (120 \text{ lbs}).$$

The total amount produced column can assist the chef in deciding how much food product to purchase. Note that the total amount produced column calculates foods in a 100 percent (edible) as served quantity. The chef would not purchase exactly 120 pounds of sirloin steak if the chef wanted to end up with 120 pounds. The chef would take into consideration the yield of the sirloin steak. The total amount of sirloin steak to be produced is 120 portions, which equals 120 pounds during the peak period.

The items per hour column indicates how many items need to be produced during one hour. To find this amount, divide the number of peak period hours into the total amount produced column:

$$120 \div 3 = 40$$

Therefore, 120 sirloin steak portions divided by 3 hours equals 40 sirloin steaks per hour.

The reason for finding the production per hour is that most equipment and equipment catalogs indicate the production capacity by the hour. A typical broiler catalog will show several models. The one you select depends on your budget and on the quantity you need to prepare. In our example, we need 40 portions of sirloin steak per hour. If you were to only broil sirloin steaks on the broiler, which would be very unlikely, you would select a broiler that would broil 40 or as close to 40 sirloin steaks as possible.

The usage time column indicates the amount of time needed to produce the food product. This time range includes the preparation and the production time. In our example, the sirloin steaks will be cut from the sirloin strip and cooked to order. The time range to prepare the steaks is from 5:00 P.M. to 6:00 P.M., and the cooked-to-order time range is the same as the peak period, from 6:00 P.M. to 9:00 P.M. The total time range is fours hours, from 5:00 P.M. to 9:00 P.M. Indicating these four hours will assist the chef in developing a production schedule. A production schedule shows who will be cooking, when the food products are to be prepared and produced, and the equipment that is needed. The sirloins steaks will be produced from 5:00 P.M. to 6:00 P.M., cooked to order from 6:00 P.M. to 9:00 P.M., and cooked on a broiler.

The remaining columns refer to the actual equipment that is needed to prepare, produce, hold, and serve the food products. The preparation column indicates the equipment that is necessary to prepare the sirloin steaks. It is at this point that you should get the food product from the storage area. In our example, the sirloin is fresh and stored in the walk-in cooler. From storage, the sirloin strip is placed on a table to be portioned. A knife and a tray or a pan are also necessary. Next, the portioned steaks are either placed back in the walk-in cooler or in a reach-in cooler near the broiler. The reach-in cooler should be indicated in the preparation column, and the broiler should be listed in the production column. The difference between the two columns is that the production equipment column indicates the major hot equipment needed during the production phase of the food product. Hot equipment usually refers to equipment such as convection ovens, fryolators, grills, steam equipment, and stoves. The holding column indicates where the food product will be held during the peak period. Cook-to-order items are usually held in a dry or refrigerated state while pre-prepared foods are held in a warm or hot state. The sirloin steaks are held in a refrigerated state. Other holding equipment items are steam tables, food warmers, and ovens.

The service column indicates the equipment that is needed to serve the food product to the customers. No additional equipment is needed to serve the sirloin steaks if the style of service used is American. If the sirloins are done table-side, you would need a réchaud and a guéridon or a portable carving cart.

The last step in analyzing equipment needs is to determine the capacity of the equipment, based on the total quantity of food that must be produced by an individual piece of equipment. The broiler is the major piece of equipment that is needed to produce the sirloin steaks. What size broiler would you need? You have to include all of the food products that will go in the broiler during the peak period. If a menu lists broiled fish, chicken, or pork products, it is necessary to add these to the number of sirloin steaks. If we need 50 orders of broiled pork chops and 120 orders of sirloin steaks, the total broiler production is 170 food items.

Next, research foodservice equipment catalogs or CDs (computer disks), and talk to a salesperson to find out which broiler model will come close to producing 170 food products per hour. By carefully studying the menu, you can better evaluate the type of equipment that is needed to produce the menu. This exercise will save you money when you are purchasing equipment.

Helpful Hints for Completing the Foodservice Equipment Analysis

- The foodservice equipment analysis is to be used only as a guideline.
- The purpose of the foodservice equipment analysis is to establish the type of foodservice equipment and the capacity of the equipment that are needed to produce the menu.
- The foodservice equipment analysis establishes a shopping list for the major, heavy-duty cooking equipment needed. Smaller pieces of equipment, such as plates, knives, and cups, should be placed on an independent list.
- Needs will vary greatly, depending on how the chef decides to purchase, prepare, store, produce, and serve food products.
- Not all columns on the equipment analysis form have to be used in the production of all products. A tossed salad does not need equipment in the production column.
- Soups, sauces, gravies, and other products with volume are usually made prior to the peak period and will not use the production column.
- Forecasting portions is a difficult task in the real job market.
- The amount of money and floor space that the chef has will greatly influence the type of equipment to be purchased.

- It is easier to use letters or numbers to represent a piece of equipment, such as the letter D to represent a mixer, than it is to write out the word *mixer* every time you need to indicate its use.
- Indicate the equipment when you use it in your planning. Some food products will use two or three pieces of equipment in the production column.

Guidelines for Designing a Hot Cooking Line

A cooking line is the heart of the kitchen. The **cooking line,** or **line,** is a grouping of the major pieces of equipment needed to cook the menu items. The layout of the line will greatly contribute to the customers' dining experience. An efficient layout allows the cook to produce menu items in an organized manner. Cooking in an organized manner allows menu items to be cooked quickly, thus providing hot food to the customers.

Using these guidelines will assist you in designing an efficient hot cooking line.

- Determine how many cooking stations will be on the line. A **cooking station** is where a particular type of cooking technique takes place, such as frying, which is done at the fry station.
- Design the work station for peak and slow production periods.
- Determine the maximum and minimum number of cooks who are needed to produce the menu items.
- Determine where the pick-up station will be prior to laying out the line.
- Analyze the percentage of work coming from each work station. Determine how many menu items are being produced from the fry station as compared to those from other stations. If 70 percent of the menu items are being produced from the fry station, then design the fry station with adequate equipment to produce 70 percent of production.
- Provide good lighting. Working in your own shadow can cause accidents.
- Provide excellent ventilation. Circulating fresh air and exhausting smoke, heat, and grease from the air keeps the cooks alert and healthy.

- Group similar and related tasks close together. When you are laying out a work station, write out every step that the cook will go through to produce a menu item. Typically, food flows through six steps: (1) receiving; (2) primary bulk storage (walk-in coolers or freezers) and/or secondary storage (reach-in refrigerators or freezers); (3) preparation (washing, peeling, cutting, chopping, etc.); (4) production (cooking the food), and holding the food for service; (5) service—serving the food to the customer; and (6) sanitation, which includes dishwashing, potwashing, and disposal. Grouping storage close to preparation or grouping preparation close to production eliminates wasted steps, motions, and time. See Figure 11-2 for a straight-line flow chart.

STRAIGHT-LINE FLOWCHART

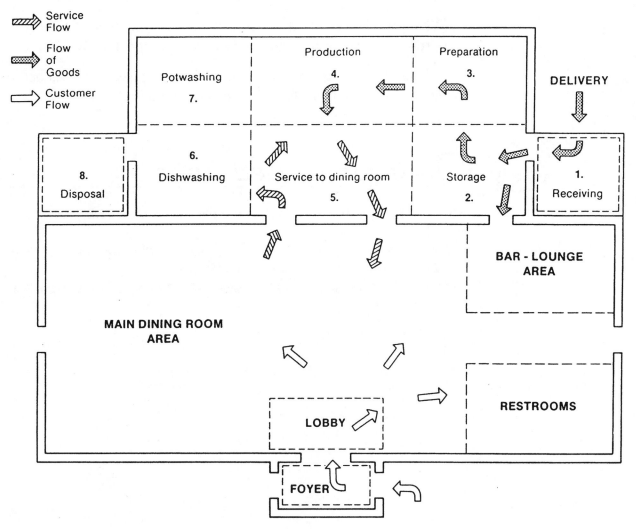

FIGURE 11-2 Straight-line Flowchart.

- When laying out the line, you must keep the front of each piece of equipment flush (even with the one next to it). Allow the back of the equipment to be uneven.

Keeping these guidelines in mind when you are laying out the line will increase productivity.

Review Questions

1. What is the difference between a guarantee and a warranty?

2. What are three guidelines you should keep in mind when you are selecting equipment?

3. What is the purpose of the foodservice equipment analysis?

4. What are four factors that will influence the number of forecasted portions you will sell in the foodservice equipment analysis?

5. Why is it important to do a foodservice equipment analysis before purchasing equipment for a foodservice operation?

Additional Readings

Edward A. Kazarian, *Foodservice Facilities Planning*, 3rd ed. (New York: John Wiley & Sons, 1989).

Lendel H. Kotschevar and Margaret E. Terrell, *Foodservice Planning: Layout and Equipment* 2nd ed. (New York: John Wiley & Sons, 1985).

Carl Scriven and James Stevens, *Food Equipment Facts.* (New York: John Wiley & Sons, 1982).

Descriptive Copy Exercise

From the following list, choose 25 menu items and describe each selection, using four adjectives for each item. Once an adjective has been used, you cannot use it again.

Breakfast Appetizers

Orange Juice   Mixed Fruit   Honeydew   Grapefruit

Breakfast Entrées

Scrambled Eggs
Western Omelette
Denver Omelette
Mushroom Omelette
Eggs Benedict
Apple Pancakes with Syrup

French Toast with Syrup
Sirloin Steak with Choice of Eggs
Corned Beef Hash with Poached
  Eggs
Waffles with Syrup
Cheese Blintzes with Fruit

Luncheon Appetizers

Nova Scotia Salmon
Oysters on the Half Shell
Antipasto

Fruit Cup with Sherbert
Marinated Herring with Sour
  Cream

Luncheon Soups

Seafood Bisque with Sherry
French Onion Soup with Cheese
Okra Chowder

Broccoli and Cheese
Minestrone
Cream of Spinach

Luncheon Salads

Chef Salad	Waldorf Salad	Cole Slaw
Spinach Salad	Crabmeat Salad	

Luncheon Entrées

Shrimp and Crabmeat au Gratin	Ground Sirloin Steak
Baked Stuffed Sole with	Chicken Divan
Newburn Sauce	Chicken Cordon Bleu
Shrimp Scampi	Chicken Kiev
Salmon with Egg Sauce	Veal Parmesan
Sautéed Brook Trout	Veal Marsala
Filet Mignon with Onion Rings	Veal Gruyère
Beef Stroganoff	Roast Turkey with Dressing
Beef Stew with Biscuit	

Luncheon Vegetables and Potatoes

Carrots with Dill	Green Beans Almandine	Scalloped Potatoes
Corn Mexican	Eggplant Parmesan	O'Brien Potatoes
Broccoli Polonaise	Mashed Potatoes	Delmonico Potatoes
Peas Forestière		

Luncheon Desserts

Pound Cake with Ice Cream	Strawberry Shortcake
Blueberry Pie with Ice Cream	Apple Crisp with Ice Cream
Pecan Pie with Whipped Cream	Chocolate Layer Cake
Boston Cream Pie	Chocolate Mousse Cake
Lemon Meringue Pie	Sundaes

Dinner Appetizers

Shrimp Cocktail	Stuffed Mushroom Caps
Escargot	Liver Paté
Shrimp Pernod	Smoked Salmon
Clams on the Half Shell	

Dinner Soups

Clam Chowder	Leak and Potato	Gazpacho
Cream of Asparagus	Scallop Bisque	

Dinner Salads

Caeser Salad
Tossed Greens

Hearts of Palm
Boston Bibb with Crabmeat

Dinner Entrées

Fettucini Alfredo
Veal Dijonnaise
Veal Picatta
Veal à la Holstein
Breast of Chicken Estragon
Roast Beef with Popovers
Chateaubriand
Broiled Lamp Chops with
   Mint Jelly
Broiled Swordfish
Baked Stuffed Shrimp

Baked Stuffed Lobster
Braised Pheasant
Roast Duckling with Cherry Sauce
Sautéed Liver with Onions
   and Bacon
Scrod Bella Vista
Lobster Thermidor
Shrimp Teriyaki
Sole Rockefeller
Seafood Brochette

Dinner Vegetables and Potatoes

Asparagus with Hollandaise
   Sauce
Glazed Carrots
Peas in Cream Sauce
Baked Stuffed Tomato
Acorn Squash
Cauliflower au Gratin

Fried Eggplant
Duchess Potatoes
Rissole Potatoes
Potato Pancakes
Sweet Potatoes
Baked Stuffed Potato

Dinner Desserts

Strawberries and Cream
Banana Cream Pie
Black Forest Cake
Lemon Chiffon Pie
Cherry Pie with Ice Cream
Rum Cake

Indian Pudding with Whipped
   Cream
Baked Alaska
Carrot Cake
Angel Food Cake

Appendix B

Descriptive Terms for Menus

A delicate wine sauce
A deliciously seasoned
A fragment mixture of
A generous portion
A gourmet's delight
An assortment of
And extraordinary ingredients
Artfully seasoned
As you prefer it
A thick, generous portion
A thick, generous treat
At its delightful perfection
Baked golden brown
Blazed in cognac
Blended with a distinctive sauce
Choice center cut
Cooked in an artistically seasoned sherry sauce
Craftily marinated
Delicately boiled and served with savory herbs
Delightfully different
Fluffy tenderness

In an intriguing blend of
In a traditional manner
Nappe with a piquante sauce
Nationally famous
Prepared according to the authentic version
Prepared to your epicurean taste
Roasted to a turn
Sauce enlivened with onions and herbs
Served in a distinctive sauce
Served steaming in a casserole
Served with a lavish hand from a bowl and tossed well to your taste
Simmered in its own juice
Taste-enriched with a perky piquante sauce
Tender, bited-sized flakes
Tender flakes
Tender sweet
Tenderly sautéed in butter
This classic French sauce
To make a meal a feast
Truly delightful
With a natural flavor

Appendix C

Words Frequently Mispelled on Students' Menus

accompaniment
avocado
bacon
banquet
barbecue sauce
béarnaise
blueberries
broccoli
burgundy
cantaloupe
cinnamon
cocktail
combination
croutons
delicate
delicious
diner
dining

fettuccini, fettucine
filet mignon
flambéed, flambé
fried
fryolator, Frialator
hollandaise
iceberg lettuce
lasagne
linguine
manicotti
mayonnaise
mozzarella
occasion
omelette, omelet
Parmesan
parsley
pimiento (pimento)

potato
prosciutto
provolone
purveyor
raisins
restaurant
ricotta
romaine
Romano
Roquefort
sprig
syrup
Tabasco
vinaigrette
vinegar
Worcestershire sauce
zucchini

Appendix D

Culinary Terms

à la Creole—In the style of Louisiana cookery; with onions, tomatoes, green peppers, and sometimes okra.

à la Florentine—Foods that have a spinach base, such as cream soup with spinach.

à la King—A white cream sauce with green peppers, pimiento, and mushrooms.

à la Mode—With ice cream.

Amandine or **Almandine**—With almonds.

au Gratin—Topped with bread crumbs and cheese, and browned.

au Jus—Served in its own juice.

Baba—Spongy yeast cake soaked in rum.

Béarnaise—An egg butter sauce in which tarragon, chervil, shallots, and meat juices have been added. Sometimes served with tenderloin.

Beaujolais—A region in the southern part of Bourgogne known for its red wines.

Béchamel—A white cream sauce made with butter, flour, and milk.

Benedict—Poached eggs with hollandaise sauce and ham or bacon, served on an English muffin.

Bisque—A creamy soup made with shellfish—usually shrimp and lobster.

Bordeaux—The most important area in France for the production of wine.

Bordelaise—A brown sauce that contains shallots, red wine, tarragon, thyme, and sometimes bone marrow.

Bortsch or **Borscht**—A vegetable soup that contains cabbage and red beets or a beef base. Originated in Russia.

Bouillabaisse—A seafood stew containing crab, mussels, sea bass, onions, tomatoes, saffron, garlic, and assorted herbs with white wine and Cognac.

Bouillon—Plain white stock originally. In today's restaurants, it is a clear soup made from fish, meat, or vegetables.

Bouquet Garni—An assortment of herbs to flavor soups, stews, or sauces.

Boursin—Cream cheese flavored with herbs and garlic. This cheese is factory made.

Brie—French cheese characterized by its white rind and rich, creamy, yellow color.

Brochette—Foods that are grilled on a skewer, for example, beef or chicken with onions, green peppers, tomatoes, and mushrooms.

Camembert—A mild, creamy flavored cheese from France.

Canapé—A small piece of bread, plain or toasted, and topped with seafood, meats, and sometimes eggs.

Capers—The pickled bud of a plant that grows in southern California and the Mediterranean Sea area, used in sauces, butter, and salads.

Caviar—The eggs of sturgeon, salmon, whitefish, and lumpfish, usually salted. The best caviar comes from Russia and Iran.

Chablis—One of the most famous dry, white wines from France.

Chantilly—A salad dressing consisting of whipped cream and mayonnaise, flavored with liquer or vanilla.

Chasseur—A garnish containing shallots, white wine, and sliced mushrooms.

Chateaubriand—A double cut of tenderloin served to two people. Served with a variety of vegetables and a border of duchess potatoes.

Cherries Jubilee—A French dessert of vanilla ice cream covered with flaming Bing cherries.

Chives—A plant that has a distinctive onion flavor and is used in salads, soups, and sour cream.

Clairet—A light red wine made in Bordeaux and Bourgogne.

Cointreau—An orange-flavored liqueur.

Compote—Stewed fruits, usually served cold.

Consommé—A clear soup, usually beef, poultry, or game, garnished with an assortment of vegetables and herbs.

Coquille Saint Jacques—A shell or shell-shaped dish that contains seafood, often with a cream sauce, topped with bread crumbs, grated cheese, and then browned.

Crepe—A thin pancake stuffed with fruits or various meats.

Croissant—A crescent-shaped pastry usually served at breakfast.

Croquettes—Usually contain fish or meat that has been chopped up and mixed with a white sauce. They are then shaped oblong, breaded, and deep fried.

Croutons—Dried pieces of bread that are cut into cubes and flavored with an array of herbs and spices. Served in salads or soups.

Demi-Glace—A rich brown sauce that has been reduced.

Demitasse—A small cup of black coffee.

Drawn Butter—Butter thta has been seasoned, usually served with fish.

Duchesse Potatoes—Mashed potatoes seasoned with nutmeg, butter, and egg yolk. Shaped and piped onto a buttered baking sheet pan.

Éclair—An oblong pastry filled with custard for dessert or with creamed food for an entrée.

Escalopes—Thinly sliced pieces of veal sautéed in fortified butter.

Espagnole—A brown sauce.

Fines Herbes—An assortment of chopped herbs, consisting of parsley, chives, chervil, and tarragon.

Fricassée—Diced veal or chicken in a white sauce.

Galantine—A dish of forcemeat, for example, galantine of duck.

Goulash—A rich beef stew that contains paprika and onions.

Hollandaise—A sauce consisting of egg yolks, butter, lemon juice, white wine, and paprika.

Hors D'oeuvre—A French word for appetizer.

Julienne—Any vegetable that is cut in a matchlike fashion, like julienne of carrots.

Kirsch—A liqueur that is distilled from fermented cherries. Used in desserts for extra flavor.

Lasagne—An Italian dish made with pasta, tomato sauce, and various cheeses.

London Broil—Marinated flank steak that is cut across the grain.

Lyonnaise—Sautéed, sliced potatoes with onions.

Macedoine—A mixture of various fruits or vegetables.

Maître D'Hôtel—Butter that contains lemon juice, white wine, parsley, and Worcestershire sauce.

Marmite—A clear broth served in an earthenware pot that usually has beef and vegetables in it.

Médaillon or **Medallion**—Small cuts of pork tenderloin or beef.

Milanaise—In the style of Milan cookery. A dish that is dipped in egg, bread crumbs, cheese, and then fried.

Minestrone—A rich Italian vegetable and pasta soup.

Mirepoix—A combination of onion, carrots, and celery. Used as a basis for sauces.

Mornay—A white cream sauce in which cheese has been added.

Mousseline—Hollandaise sauce in which whipped cream has been added.

Napoleon—Squares cut from puff pastry filled with cream.

Newburg—A cream sauce in which egg yolk and sherry have been added to enrich the taste.

Normande—A sauce made from white wine and cream, served with fish.

O'Brien Potatoes—Potatoes that are diced and cooked, then sautéed with green peppers, pimientos, and bacon.

(à la) Parisienne—Garnish for chicken or fish consisting of mushroom, asparagus, truffles, with a white wine sauce.

Pâté—A mixture of meat, usually pork, fish, or game. Baked in an earthenware dish or in a pastry case, usually served cold.

Petit Four—A small cake or pastry.

Provençale—Cooking style of the southern province of France, consisting of tomato sauce, garlic, herbs, and olives.

Ragout—Brown or white stew usually with a small amount of red sauce.

Ravioli—An Italian pasta dish filled with meat, vegatables, or cheese.

Robert—A sauce made with onions, mustard, white wine, and vinegar. Often served with roast pork.

Roulade—Rolled meat or fish stuffed with vegetables.

Shallot—A member of the onion family.

Shish Kabob, or **Shish Kebab**—Beef, lamb, chicken, or fish roasted on a skewer, served with tomatoes, green peppers, onions, and mushrooms.

Smitane—A sauce made of white wine and sour cream.

Sole—Delicate-tasting fish that is flat. The true sole, English Dover sole, is found only in Europe.

Spumoni—Ice cream that is flavored with fruit. Originated in Italy.

Steak Tartare—Tenderloin that has been minced, seasoned, and reshaped. It is often served with raw onions, capers, and egg yolk. The meat is served raw.

Torte—A rich cake layered with cream.

Tournedos—Small rounded steak from the thickest part of the fillet.

Truffe or **Truffle**—A black fungus that is similar to a mushroom and grows underground. It is used as a garnish, for the most part, because of its high price.

Turbot—A fish that is similar to halibut. It is flat in nature.

Vacherin—A dessert that has meringue and whipped cream on a pastry.

Velouté—A creamy white sauce that is made from white stock.

Vermicelli—A thin pasta used in consommé.

Vichyssoise—A soup made of potatoes or leeks, from France.

Vinaigrette—A cold dressing made of oil and vinegar, herbs, spices, and lemon juice.

Vol-Au-Vent—A puff pastry filled with an array of creamed foods.

Wiener Schnitzel—Veal that has been breaded and sautéed, garnished with anchovy, caper, and a lemon slice.

Yorkshire Pudding—Popover pastry usually served with roast beef. Originated in England.

Appendix E

Measurements

General Equivalents

16 tablespoons	=	1 cup
1 cup (standard measure)	=	½ pint (8 fluid ounces)
2 cups	=	1 pint
16 ounces	=	1 pound
3 quarts (dry)	=	1 peck
4 pecks	=	1 bushel
32 ounces	=	1 fluid quart
128 ounces = 8 pounds	=	1 fluid gallon
1 No. 10 can	=	13 cups
1 pound margarine	=	2 cups
1 pound flour	=	4 cups

The number of the scoop determines the number of servings in each quart of a mixture; that is, with a No. 16 scoop, one quart of mixture will yield 16 servings.

Decimal Equivalents of Fractions

0.25 = ¼		0.66 = ⅔	
0.33 = ⅓		0.75 = ¾	
0.5 = ½			

The abbreviation beside the fraction tells what unit of measure to use.

Appendix F

A Practical Guide to the Nutrition Labeling Laws for the Restaurant Industry*

Foodservice Operations: Making Nutrient Content Claims

Although restaurant food is generally exempted from nutrition labeling requirements, nutrient claims made by restaurateurs are regulated under NLEA. A nutrient content claim is a word or phrase used to describe the level of a nutrient in a particular food or dish. There are three types of claims described in the following section. If you make one of these types of claims in advertising, on promotional materials or on a menu, that food item must meet the specific FDA definition.

---

*Prepared as a Member Service by Donna Shields, MS, RD, for the National Restaurant Association.

Absolute Claims

An absolute claim is a statement made about the exact amount or range of a nutrient in a food. "Low fat" and "calorie free" are examples of absolute claims. Definitions of these terms are not required to appear in print, in the ad, on the menu or promotional materials, but the food must meet the specific criteria.

Relative or Comparative Claims

A relative or comparative claim is a statement that compares the amount of a nutrient in a food with the amount of that nutrient in a reference food. Claims such as "light," "reduced" and "less" are examples of relative claims.

A reference food may be the restaurant's regular product, or another restaurant's product, that has been offered for sale to the public on a regular basis for a substantial period of time. Nutrient values for a reference food may also be derived from a valid database, an average of top national or regional brands, or a market basket norm. A "reduced" claim may only be used to compare individual foods that are similar. "More" or "less" claims, however, may be used to compare any foods within the same product category (e.g., potato chips and pretzels).

Definitions of relative claims are not required to appear in print, in the ad, on the menu or promotional materials, but the food must meet the specific criteria. The criteria include a comparison of the two foods, the percentage of reduction and the actual nutrient content of both foods.

Implied Claims

An implied claim is a statement made that implies that a nutrient is present or absent in a food. Such claims often use an ingredient name that implies the inclusion or absence of a nutrient. "High in oat bran" implies the food is high in fiber, which means the food must meet the criteria for a "high fiber" claim. There is a fair amount of gray area relating to implied claims, and FDA has determined it will review questions that arise on a case-by-case basis. The context in which a statement is made can alter its meaning. You must use good judgment when writing menu or advertising copy. For example, consider the claim, "Made with whole wheat flour." Are you implying that the fiber content of this dish is higher because of the whole wheat flour or are you simply stating an ingredient? This question is open to interpretation.

Statements That Are Not Nutrient Claims

FDA does not consider all statements that describe the content of a food to be nutrient content claims. FDA will examine the context in which the statement appears to determine if a nutrient content claim is implied. For example, if promotional materials highlighted a restaurant's oat bran muffins and the display bore a bright banner with "oat bran" in large, bright letters, the emphasis on "oat bran" probably would cause FDA to view the materials as making an implied "good source" claim for fiber. The rules in this area, however, leave room for interpretation. People, therefore, may reasonably disagree as to whether a particular statement constitutes a nutrient content claim.

Generally, statements that pertain to the inclusion or absence of ingredients having a perceived value are not considered nutrient content claims. For example:

- Contains no MSG
- Contains no milk or milk fat
- Made with whole fruit and honey

Statements in which an ingredient is part of the identity of the food are not considered nutrient content claims. For example:

- Whole wheat pasta
- Multigrain bread

If you identify such items with a symbol, to denote some nutritional benefit or make other claims, however, you may be making an implied claim and must explain it and meet the appropriate criteria.

Nutrient Content Claims

All nutrient content claims are based on Reference Amounts of food. Reference Amounts are standardized serving sizes, as determined by FDA, that must be used as the basis for nutrient content claims, as well as health claims. These amounts represent the average and customary amount of a given food typically consumed at one time. The Reference Amounts for foods, main dishes and meals appear on pages 27-32.

You will need to refer to the Reference Amount chart to interpret the following nutrient content claim terms. Working with Reference Amounts means becoming familiar with gram weights of food products, but gram weights are easy to determine with an electronic digital scale.

Substantiation for any nutrient content claims must be available, in written form, for customers, upon request.

The following is a list of terms, established by FDA, to be used when making nutrient content claims. The description accompanying each term defines the criteria that a food must meet in order to use the term. As you will see, this is where Reference Amounts come into play. Under wording options, alternatives for some of the terms are also given. Remember: terms that are not defined by FDA may not be used to characterize the level of nutrient content in a food.

Calories

Free   Less than 5 calories per Reference Amount.

Wording Options:
Free of Calories
No Calories
Zero Calories
Without Calories
Trivial Source of Calories

Low   40 calories or less per Reference Amount when Reference Amount is 30 grams or more, or more than 2 tablespoons.

Food with Reference Amounts of 30 grams or less or 2 tablespoons or less, such as olives, croutons, grated cheese, can be called "low calorie" only if they contain 40 calories or less per 50 grams. This prevents a "low calorie" claim being based on a small amount of food.

For main dish items and meals, 120 calories or less per 100 grams. (See definitions on page 34.)

Wording Options:
Low in Calories
Low Source of Calories
Few Calories
Contains a Small Amount of Calories

Reduced   Minimum of 25 percent fewer calories per Reference Amount.

For main dish items and meals, minimum of 25 percent fewer calories per 100 grams.

This claim may not be made if the food to which comparison is being made meets the criteria for "low calorie."

Example: Reduced calorie blueberry coffee cake, with 25 percent fewer calories than a standard blueberry coffee cake recipe. Calorie content has been reduced from 200 to 150 calories per serving.

Wording Options:
Lower Calorie
Fewer Calories
Calorie Reduced

Light/Lite

If food derives less than 50 percent of its calories from fat, 1/3 fewer calories or 50 percent less fat per Reference Amount. If food derives greater than 50 percent or more of its calories from fat, 50 percent less fat per Reference Amount.

Example: Our lite rice pudding has 100 calories per serving compared to a standard rice pudding recipe with 150 calories.

For main dish items and meals, meet the requirements for low calorie or low fat and identify nature of the claim.

Example: A lite chicken stir fry with brown rice, a low calorie meal. (See definition of low calorie meal.)

The words "light" or "lite" may be used for other descriptions, such as "Lite Bites" referring to smaller portion sizes. If so, explanation must appear with, or in close proximity to, the statement.

Alternative Usage:
Light in Color
Light in Texture
Lightly Flavored
Light Bites (smaller portion sizes)
Light Corn Syrup (statement of identity)

Fat

Free

Less than 0.5 grams of fat per Reference Amount and per serving.

For main dish items and meals, less than 0.5 grams of fat per serving size.

Consistent with FDA's labeling requirements for packaged foods, restaurateurs should be prepared to identify on request any ingredient that adds a trivial amount of fat to the food, main dish, or meal that is the subject of the claim.

Wording Options:
Free of Fat
Nonfat
No Fat
Zero Fat
Without Fat
Trivial Source of Fat
Negligible Source of Fat

Low   3 grams of fat or less per Reference Amount when Reference Amount is greater than 30 grams, or more than 2 tablespoons.

Foods with Reference Amounts of 30 grams or less or 2 tablespoons or less, such as olives, croutons, grated cheese, can be called "low fat" only if they contain 3 grams of fat or less per Reference Amount and per 50 grams. This prevents "low fat" claims from being based on a small amount of food.

For main dish items and meals, must contain 3 grams of fat or less per 100 grams and not more than 30 percent of calories from fat.

Wording Options:
Low in Fat
Little Fat
Low Source of Fat
Contains a Small Amount of Fat

Reduced   Minimum of 25 percent less fat per Reference Amount.

For main dish items and meals, minimum of 25 percent less fat per 100 grams.

This claim may not be made if the food to which it is being compared meets the criteria for "low fat."

Example: Reduced fat chocolate cake has 30 percent less fat than a standard chocolate cake recipe. Fat content has been reduced from 10 grams to 7 grams.

Wording Options:
Lower in Fat
Lower Fat
Less Fat
Fat Reduced
Reduced in Fat

Light/Lite   If food derives greater than 50 percent or more of its calories from fat, 50 percent less fat per Reference Amount. If the food derives less than 50 percent of its calories from fat, 50 percent less fat or 1/3 fewer calories per Reference Amount.

Example: This lite blue cheese dressing has 50 percent less fat than a standard blue cheese dressing recipe. Fat has been reduced from 10 grams to 5 grams per serving.

Saturated Fat

Free   Less than 0.5 grams of saturated fat and less than 0.5 grams trans fatty acid per Reference Amount and per serving.

For main dish items and meals, less than 0.5 grams of saturated fat and less than 0.5 grams trans fatty acid per serving.

Consistent with FDA's labeling requirements for packaged foods, restaurateurs should be prepared to identify on request any ingredient that adds a trivial amount of saturated fat to the food, main dish, or meal that is the subject of the claim.

Wording Options:
No Saturated Fat
Zero Saturated Fat
Without Saturated Fat
Free of Saturated Fat

Low   1 gram of saturated fat or less per Reference Amount and no more than 15 percent of calories from saturated fat.

For main dish items and meals, must contain 1 gram of saturated fat or less per 100 grams and less than 10 percent of calories from saturated fat.

Wording Options:
Low in Saturated Fat
Low Source of Saturated Fat
A Little Saturated Fat
Contains a Small Amount of Saturated Fat

Reduced   Minimum of 25 percent less saturated fat per Reference Amount.

For main dish items and meals, minimum of 25 percent less saturated fat per 100 grams.

This claim may not be made if the food to which it is being compared meets the definition of "low saturated fat."

Example: This Garden Omelet is lower in saturated fat than a standard vegetable omelet receipe. Saturated fat has been reduced 50 percent from 6 grams to 3 grams.

Wording Options:
Less Saturated Fat
Lowered Saturated Fat
Reduced in Saturated Fat
Lowered in Saturated Fat

Cholesterol

Free   Less than 2 milligrams of cholesterol per Reference Amount and per serving and 2 grams or less of saturated fat per Reference Amount.

For main dish items and meals, contains less than 2 milligrams of cholesterol and 2 grams or less of saturated fat per serving.

If the total fat content of a food, main dish, or meal exceeds the following levels when making a cholesterol free claim, you must declare the total amount of fat next to the claim.
Per Reference Amount
Food = more than 13 grams per serving
Main dish = more than 19.5 grams
Meal = more than 26 grams

Consistent with FDA's labeling requirements for packaged foods, restaurateurs should be prepared to identify on request any ingredients that add a trivial amount of cholesterol to the food, main dish, or meal that is the subject of the claim.

Example: Cholesterol free French fries. Contains _____ grams of fat per serving. (If potatoes are fried in a vegetable oil, they are still a fairly high fat food. If your particular finished product contains more than 13 grams of fat per Reference Amount, you must declare the fat content in grams.) This type of regulation guards against customers being misled into thinking "cholesterol free" is synonymous with low fat.

Wording Options:
Zero Cholesterol
No Cholesterol

Free of Cholesterol
Without Cholesterol
Trivial Source of Cholesterol

Low   20 milligrams or less of cholesterol and 2 grams or less of saturated fat per Reference Amount. Must also contain 13 grams or less of total fat per Reference Amount.

Foods with Reference Amounts less than 30 grams or less than 2 tablespoons, such as croutons or grated cheese, can be called "low cholesterol" only if they meet the above criteria based on the Reference Amount and on a 50 gram basis. This prevents a "low cholesterol" claim from being based on the small amount of food.

For main dish items, must contain 20 milligrams of cholesterol or less and 2 grams of saturated fat or less per 100 grams and 19.5 grams or less of total fat per serving.

For meals, must contain 20 milligrams or less of cholesterol and 2 grams or less of saturated fat per 100 grams and 26 grams or less of total fat per serving.

When fat content exceeds the listed criteria, the total fat content in grams must be declared.

Example: Low cholesterol pound cake. This pound cake contains 15 grams of fat per serving. (If a recipe has replaced butter and eggs with vegetable oil, lowering cholesterol but maintaining a fat content higher than 13 grams, then the fat content declaration must be made).

Wording Options:
Low in Cholesterol
Little Cholesterol
Contains a Small Amount of Cholesterol

Reduced   Minimum of 25 percent less cholesterol and 2 grams or less of saturated fat per Reference Amount and 13 grams or less of total fat per Reference Amount and per serving (and per 50 grams if the Reference Amount is 30 grams or less or 2 tablespoons or less).

For main dish items, minimum of 25 percent less cholesterol and 2 grams or less of saturated fat per 100 grams and 19.5 grams of total fat or less per serving.

For meals, minimum of 25 percent less cholesterol and 2 grams or less of saturated fat per 100 grams and 26 grams of total fat or less per serving.

When fat exceeds listed criteria, fat content in grams must be declared.

Example: This cholesterol reduced seafood Newburg has 30 percent less cholesterol than a standard seafood Newburg recipe. Cholesterol has been reduced from 80 mg to 55 mg of cholesterol per serving.

Wording Options:
Less Cholesterol
Lower Cholesterol
Reduced in Cholesterol
Lower in Cholesterol

Sodium

Free   Less than 5 milligrams of sodium per Reference Amount and per serving.

For main dish items and meals, must contain less than 5 milligrams of sodium per serving.

Consistent with FDA's labeling requirements for packaged foods, restaurateurs should be prepared to identify on request any ingredients that add a trivial amount of sodium to the food, main dish, or meal that is the subject of the claim.

Wording Options:
No Sodium
Zero Sodium
Without Sodium
Free of Sodium
Trivial Source of Sodium

Low   140 milligrams or less of sodium per Reference Amount when Reference Amount is 30 grams or more, or more than 2 tablespoons. When Reference Amount is 30 grams or less or 2 tablespoons or less, use same criteria based on Reference Amount and 50 grams.

For main dish items and meals, must contain 140 milligrams or less of sodium per 100 grams.

Very Low   35 milligrams or less of sodium based on above criteria.

Wording Options:
Very Low in Sodium

Reduced Minimum of 25 percent less sodium per Reference Amount.

For main dish items and meals, minimum of 25 percent less sodium per 100 grams.

This claim may not be made if the food to which it is compared meets the requirements for "low sodium."

Example: Made with a reduced sodium soy sauce—50 percent less sodium than regular soy sauce. Sodium content has been reduced from 700 mg to 350 mg per serving.

Wording Options:
Reduced in Sodium
Less Sodium
Lower Sodium
Lower in Sodium

Light in Sodium/
Lite in Sodium Minimum of 50 percent less sodium per Reference Amount.

For main dish items and meals, must meet the criteria for low sodium.

Salt Free Meet criteria for sodium free.

Unsalted
No Salt Added
Without Added Salt These terms are allowed if:

- there is no salt added during preparation
- the food it resembles is normally prepared with salt

If the food does not meet the criteria for a sodium free food, a declaration statement, "not a sodium free food" or "not for the control of sodium in the diet" appears near the claim

Lightly Salted Minimum of 50 percent less sodium added than is normally used in preparation. If a food does not meet the criteria for a "low sodium" food, a declaration statement, "not a low sodium food," must appear near the claim.

Remember, salt and sodium are not the same and you cannot use these words interchangeably. Salt refers to sodium chloride, which is composed of 40 percent sodium. It is the sodium content of a food that is the basis for nutrient content claims.

Sugar

Free   Less than 0.5 grams of sugar per Reference Amount and per serving.

For main dish items and meals, must have 0.5 grams or less of sugar per serving.

If the food is not labeled "low calorie" or "reduced calorie," a declaration statement, "not a low calorie food" or "not a reduced calorie food," must appear near the claim.

Consistent with FDA's labeling requirements for packaged foods, restaurateurs should be prepared to identify on request any ingredients that add a trivial amount of sugar to the food, main dish, or meal that is the subject of the claim.

Wording Options:
Free of Sugar
Sugarless
No Sugar
Zero Sugar
Without Sugar
Trivial Source of Sugar

Low   Cannot be used as a claim.

Reduced   Minimum of 25 percent less sugar per Reference Amount.

For main dish items and meals, minimum of 25 percent less sugar per 100 grams.

Example: Our reduced sugar lemonade has 25 percent less sugar than a standard lemonade recipe. Sugar content has been reduced from 8 to 6 grams per serving.

Wording Options:
Reduced in Sugar
Less Sugar
Lower Sugar
Sugar Reduced
Lower in Sugar

No Added Sugar
No Sugar Added
Without Added
Sugar   These terms are allowed if:

- no sugar or ingredient that contains added sugar, such as jam, jelly, concentrated fruit juice has been added during preparation
- the food it resembles normally uses sugar in the preparation

If the food does not meet the criteria for a low calorie or reduced calorie food, a declaration statement, "not a low calorie food" or "not a reduced calorie food" must appear near the claim.

Other Nutrient Content Claim Terms You Need To Know

Provides
Contains
Good Source

To use these terms, the food must contain 10 to 19 percent of the Daily value per Reference Amount. These terms cannot be used to make a total carbohydrate claim. Refer to the Daily Value chart on page 46 for information concerning the Daily Values for specific nutrients.

If using these terms to describe a main dish or meal, identify the food component that is the subject of the claim.

Example: The black-eyed peas in this meal provide fiber.

High
Excellent Source Of
Rich In

To use these terms, the food must contain 20 percent or more of the Daily Value per Reference Amount. Refer to the chart on page 46 for information concerning the Daily Values for specific nutrients.

If using these terms to describe a main dish or meal, identify the food component that is the subject of the claim.

Example: The fruit compote in our breakfast special is an excellent source of vitamin C.

More
Added
Enriched
Fortified

To use these terms, the food must contain at least 10 percent more of the Daily Value for protein, vitamins, minerals, fiber or potassium per Reference Amount compared to the reference food.

Example: These apple bran muffins contain 25 percent more fiber than our regular apple muffins. Fiber content of an apple muffin is 3 grams per serving; apple bran muffin is 4 grams per serving.

If using these terms to describe a main dish or meal, use the above criteria based on 100 grams of product.

"Fortified" and "enriched" cannot be used to describe single ingredient meat or poultry products.

Fiber	To make any fiber claim, the food must meet the criteria for either "good source" or "high." If the food is not "low fat," you must declare the fat content per serving.
Lean	To use this term for meat, poultry, seafood, and game, food must have less than 10 grams of fat, less than 4 grams of saturated fat, and less than 95 milligrams per Reference Amount and 100 grams.
	If using this term to describe a main dish or meal, use the above criteria based on 100 grams and serving size.
Extra Lean	To use this term for meat, poultry, seafood, and game, food must have less than 5 grams of fat, less than 2 grams of saturated fat, and less than 95 milligrams of cholesterol per Reference Amount and 100 grams.
	If using this term to describe a main dish or meal, use the above criteria based on 100 grams and serving size.
Fresh	When "fresh" is used in a manner that implies that the product is unprocessed, the food must be in its raw state and not have undergone freezing, thermal treatment, or any other form of preservation. Apart from this restriction, terms such as "fresh," "freshly prepared," and "freshly baked" should be used in a truthful and non-misleading manner. The use of these terms will be reviewed on a case-by-case basis.
Natural	There is no set definition or regulation governing the use of this word. Current FDA policy, however, treats a claim of "natural" as meaning that nothing artificial or synthetic has been included in the food that would not normally be expected to be in the food.
Healthy	To use this term, a food must be low fat, low in saturated fat, contain 480 milligrams or less of sodium per serving, and provide at least 10 percent of the Daily Value per Reference Amount for protein, fiber, iron, calcium, vitamins A or C. Seafood or game meats must have 5 grams or less of fat and 2 grams or less of saturated fat per Reference

Amount and 100 grams, and 95 milligrams or less of cholesterol per 100 grams. The sodium and other nutrient criteria are the same.

Raw fruits or vegetables are exempted from the requirement that "healthy" foods provide at least 10 percent of the Daily Value per Reference Amount for the above-referenced nutrients.

If using this term to describe meals or main dishes, they must be low fat, low in saturated fat, and have 600 milligrams or less of sodium and 90 milligrams or less of cholesterol per serving. A main dish must contain 10 percent of the Daily Value for 2 nutrients, and, for meals, 3 nutrients.

Reference Manuals

There are numerous books that contain nutritional value information for a wide variety of foods. The following publications are ones that dietitians and nutrition professionals use and are to be considered reliable and comprehensive sources.

Bowes and Church's *Food Values of Portions Commonly Used.* Anna DePlanter Bowes, rev. by Jean A.T. Pennington. 16th edition, J.B. Lippincott, Philadelphia, 1994.

Composition of Foods: Raw, Processed and Prepared. Agriculture Handbook No. 8. Agricultural Research Service, U.S. Department of Agriculture, 1976.

Convenience Food Facts: Help for Planning Quick, Healthy, and Convenient Meals. A. Monk, DCI/Chronimed Publishing, Minneapolis, 1991.

Dr. Jean Mayer's Diet and Nutrition Guide. J. Mayer, Pharos Books, New York, 1990.

Everything About Exchange Values for Foods. M. Swanson and P. Cinnamon, University Press of Idaho, Moscow, 1986.

Fast Food Facts: Nutrition and Exchange Values for Fast-Food Restaurants. M. Franz, DCI Publishing, 1990.

Foods of Hawaii and the Pacific Basin. N. Wenkam, Hawaii Institute of Tropical Agriculture and Human Resources, Honolulu 1980.

Nutrient Values of Muscle Foods: Composition Values for Specific Cuts of Beef. National Livestock and Meat Board, Chicago, 1990.

The Complete Book of Food Counts. C. Netzer, Dell Publishing, New York, 1991.

References

Browne, M. *Label Facts for Healthful Eating.* National Food Processors Association, 1993.

Federal Register. Vol 58, No. 3. January 6, 1993 (2 books). Food and Drug Administration, Food Labeling Rule; and Food Safety and Inspection Service, Nutrition Labeling Rules.

Federal Register. Vol. 59, No. 89. 21 CFR Part 101. May 10, 1994. Food and Drug Administration, Definition of Term: Healthy; Final Rule.

Gourmet News. "Small Business Labeling Exemptions." April 1994.

U.S. Department of Agriculture, National Agricultural Library, Food and Nutrition Information Center. Microcomputer Software Collection. December 1993.

U.S. Department of Health and Human Services, *Questions and Answers, Volume II, A Guide for Restaurants and Other Retail Establishments.* August 1995.

Appendix G

National Restaurant Association's Accuracy in Menus*

Accuracy in Menus offers foodservice operators specific guidelines for the proper representation of products served. Truthful representation involves more than just item description. Photographs, graphic illustrations, printed advertisements and verbal depiction by employees must also be accurately presented. This guide outlines some common misrepresentations which can be easily avoided by clarification of terms.

Customer satisfaction and prevention of government intervention depends on accuracy in menu offerings. Care should be taken that all written or spoken words are substantiated with product, invoice or label.

*"Accuracy in Menus," Copyright © 1984 by National Restaurant Association, Washington, D.C.

Representation of Quantity

Proper operational procedures should preclude any misinterpretations regarding size or quantity.

Steaks are often merchandised by weight. It is generally assumed that declared weight is that prior to cooking and can be safely listed as such. "Jumbo" eggs should mean exactly that, since Jumbo is a recognized egg standard (30 ounces). Similarly, "Petite" and "Super Colossal" are official size descriptions for olives. Check with your suppliers for official standards or purchase a copy of *Specs, The Comprehensive Foodservice Purchasing and Specification Manual*, published by CBI Publishing Company, Inc., Boston, MA.

Although double martinis are obviously twice the size of the normal drink, the use of terms such as "extra large drink" should be verified. Also, remember the implied meaning of words: a bowl of soup contains more than a cup of soup.

Representation of Quality

Federal and state standards of quality grades exist for many restaurant products, including meat, poultry, eggs, dairy products, fruits and vegetables. Terminology used to describe grades include Prime, Grade A, Good, No. 1, Choice, Fancy, Grade AA and Extra Standard.

Menu descriptions which use these words may imply certain quality and must be accurate. An item appearing as "Choice sirloin of beef" connotes the use of USDA Choice Grade sirloin of beef. The term "prime rib" is an exception to this rule; prime rib is a long established, accepted description for a cut of beef (the "prime" ribs, the sixth to twelfth ribs) and does not represent the grade quality unless USDA is used in conjunction.

The USDA definition of ground beef is just what the name implies. No extra fat, water, extenders or binders are permitted. The fat limit is 30 percent. Seasonings may be added as long as they are identified. These requirements identify only product ground and packaged in federal or state-inspected plants.

Representation of Price

If your pricing structure includes a cover charge, service charge or gratuity, these must be appropriately brought to your customers' attention. If extra charges are made for requests, such as "all white meat" or "no ice drinks," these should also be stated at the time of ordering.

Any coupon or premium promotion restrictions must be clearly defined.

If a price promotion involves a multi-unit company, clearly indicate which units are participating.

Representation of Brand Names

Any brand name product that is advertised must be the one served. A registered or copywritten trademark or brand name must not be used generically to refer to a product. Several examples of brand name restaurant products are:

Armour Bacon, Sanka, Log Cabin Syrup, Coca-Cola, Seven-Up, Swift Premium Ham, Pepsi-Cola, Starkist Tuna, Ry-Krisp, Jello, Heinz Catsup, Maxwell House Coffee, Folgers Coffee, Kraft Cheese, Tabasco Sauce, Ritz Crackers, Seven and Seven and Miracle Whip.

Your own house brand of a product may be so labeled, even when prepared by an outside source if its manufacturing was to your specification.

Representation of Product Identification

Substituting one food item for another is common. These substitutions may be due to nondelivery, availability, merchandising considerations or price. Menus must accurately specify all subsitions that are made. Common examples are:

Maple syrup and maple-flavored syrup
Boiled ham and baked ham
Chopped and shaped veal pattie and veal cutlet
Standard ice cream and French-style ice cream

Cod and haddock
Noodles and egg noodles
Light meat tuna and white meat tuna
Milk and skim milk
Pure jams and pectin jams
Whipped topping and whipped cream
Turkey and chicken
Hereford beef and Black Angus beef
Peanut oil and corn oil
Beef liver and calves' liver
Ice Milk and ice cream
Powdered eggs and fresh eggs
Picnic-style pork shoulder and ham
Ground beef and ground sirloin of beef
Capon and chicken
Cream and half & half
Margarine and butter
Nondairy creamers or whiteners and cream
Pollack and haddock
Flounder and sole
Cheese food and processed cheese
Cream sauce and nondairy cream sauce
Bonito and tuna fish
Roquefort cheese and blue cheese
Tenderloin tips and diced beef
Mayonnaise and salad dressing

Representation of Points of Origin

Products identified by their points of origin must be authentic. Claims may be substantiated by packaging labels, invoices or other documentation provided by the product's supplier. Mistakes are possible as sources of supply change and availability of product shifts. The following are common assertions of points of origin:

Lake Superior whitefish   Danish blue cheese
Idaho potatoes   Louisiana frog legs
Maine lobster   Florida stone crabs
Imported Swiss cheese   Chesapeake Bay oysters
Puget Sound sockeye salmon   Colorado brook trout
Bay scallops   Alaskan king crab

Gulf shrimp
Florida orange juice
Smithfield ham
Wisconsin cheese

Imported ham
Long Island duckling
Colorado beef

There is widespread use of geographic names used in a generic sense to describe methods of preparation or service. Such terminology is commonly understood and accepted by the customer and need not be restricted. Examples are:

Russian dressing
French toast
New England clam chowder
Country fried steak
Irish stew
Danish pastries
German potato salad
Russian service
French service

Denver sandwich
Country ham
French dip
French fries
Swiss steak
English muffins
Manhattan clam chowder
Swiss cheese

Representation of Merchandising Terms

Exaggerations in advertising are acceptable if they do not mislead. "We serve the best gumbo in town" is understood by consumers for what it is—boasting for advertising's sake. However, "We use only the finest beef" implies that USDA Prime beef is used since a standard exists for this product. Similarly, a customer who orders a "mile-high pie" would expect it to be heaped with a fluffy topping. However, to advertise a "foot-long hotdog" and then serve something less would be in error.

Mistakes are possible in properly identifying steak cuts. The National Association of Meat Purveyors' *Meat Buyer's Guide* lists industry standards which should be used.

Since most foodservice sanitation ordinances prohibit the preparation of foods in home facilities, the term "homemade" should not be used when describing menu offerings. "Homestyle," "homemade style," or "our own" are suggested alternatives.

Use of the following terms should be verifiable:

Fresh daily
Fresh roasted
Flown in daily

Corn-fed porkers
Slept in Chesapeake Bay
Finest quality

Kosher meat	Center-cut ham
Black Angus beef	Own special sauce
Aged steaks	Low calorie
Milk-fed chicken	

Representation of Means of Preservation

Menus often list foods which have been canned, chilled, bottled, frozen or dehydrated. If these terms are used to describe menu selections, they must be accurate. Frozen orange juice is not fresh, canned peas are not frozen and bottled applesauce is not canned.

Representation of Food Preparation

The means of food preparation is often the determining factor in the customer's selection of a menu entrée. Absolute accuracy is a must. Readily understood terms include:

Charcoal-broiled	Roasted
Stir-fried	Poached
Sauteed	Fried in butter
Deep-fried	Mesquite-grilled
Baked	Grilled
Smoked	Steamed
Broiled	Rotisseried
Prepared from scratch	Barbecued

Representation of Verbal and Visual Presentation

Menus, wall placards or other advertising which contain a pictorial representation of a meal or platter must not be misleading. Examples of visual misrepresentation include:

- mushroom caps pictured in a sauce when mushroom pieces are actually used

- whole strawberries pictured on a shortcake when sliced strawberries are actually used
- single thick slice of meat pictured when numerous thin slices are actually used
- six shrimp pictured when five shrimp are actually used
- vegetables or other extras pictured with a meal when they are not actually included
- a sesame seed-topped bun pictured when a plain bun is actually used

Servers must also provide accurate descriptions of products. Examples of verbal misrepresentations include:

- the question "Would you like sour cream or butter with your potatoes?" when in fact an imitation sour cream or margarine is served
- the statement "The pies are baked in our kitchen" when in fact the pies were baked elsewhere

Appendix H

Menu Marketing Characteristics

Marketing Characteristics	Good Menus	Common Mistakes
Size	Large enough to read; small enough to handle	Too small; too large
Descriptive copy	For each item	Not enough descriptive copy
Printing	*No reverse type;* large enough to read; uppercase for headings and subheadings	Headings and subheadings not in uppercase; too small; too much type; too crowded
Listing	Items listed in order eaten; profitable items first and last in a column	Clip-ons cover other specials; omission of liquor or desserts; in wrong order; listing entrées on left; low-profit items listed first
Cover	Fits decor	Back cover not used
Visibility	Proper lighting	Not enough light

Appendix I

Menu-Making Principles

Before a menu is made, the following should be analyzed:

Type of customer	Adequacy of equipment
Location	Sales volume
Hours of service	Markets
Type of operation	Competition
Capacity and condition of kitchen	Season
Skill and capability of kitchen crew	Occasion
Skill and experience of foodservice crew	Cost and profits

Know your foods. Get acquainted with grades, varieties, and differences in the following classifications:

Meats—fresh and processed

Poultry—fresh and frozen

Vegetables—canned, fresh, and frozen

Fruits—fresh, preserved, frozen, and canned

Dairy products—pasteurized and graded

Condiments and relishes

Flour—cereals and mixes

Beverages—coffee, tea, and cocoa

Groceries—spices and seasonings

To satisfy guests, the menu planner must consider the following:

Turnover	Texture
Leftovers	Color
On-hand supplies	Arrangement
Variety	Speed of service
Balance	Merchandising
Temperature	Weather
Season	

Know how your kitchen operates. Be familiar with the personnel and the equipment, and the function of each.

Chef = manager

Sous chef = principal assistant

Saucier = sauce cook

Garde manger = cold cook

Poissonier = seafood cook

Rotisseur = roasting cook

Entremetier = vegetable cook

Boucher = butcher

Potager = soup cook

Understand the task that each of these individuals performs, and do not plan a menu that will overwork any one station.

Bibliography

"A Road Map for 2000," *Restaurant Institution,* 1 January 2000, 66–74.

Klaus Boehm, Brian Chadwick, and Fay Sharman, *The Taste of France.* (Boston: Houghton Mifflin, 1982).

Paul R. Dittmer and Gerald G. Griffin, *Principles of Food, Beverage, and Labor Cost Controls,* 6th ed. (New York: John Wiley & Sons, 1999).

Karen Eich Drummond, *Nutrition for the Foodservice Professional,* 4th ed. (New York: John Wiley & Sons, 2001).

John A. Drysdale, *Profitable Menu Planning.* (Englewood Cliffs, NJ: Prentice-Hall, 1994).

Wayne Gisslen, *Professional Cooking,* 4th ed. (New York: John Wiley & Sons, 1999).

Mary B. Grosvenor and Lori A. Smolin, *Nutrition Science and Application,* 2nd ed. (Fort Worth, TX: Saunders College Publishing, 1994).

Sandy Kapoor, *Professional Healthy Cooking.* (New York: John Wiley & Sons, 1995).

Edward A. Kazarian, *Food Service Facilities Planning,* 3rd ed. (New York: John Wiley & Sons, 1989).

Lendal H. Kotschevar and Margaret E. Terrell, *Food Service Planning: Layout and Equipment,* 2nd ed. (New York: John Wiley & Sons, 1985).

Lendal H. Kotschevar and Marcel R. Escoffier, *Management by Menu,* 3rd ed. (Chicago, IL: Educational Foundation of the National Restaurant Association, 1994).

Lothar A. Kreck, *Menus: Analysis and Planning,* 2nd ed. (New York: Van Nostrand Reinhold, 1984).

Sarah R. Labensky and Alan M. Hause, *On Cooking Techniques from Expert Chefs.* (Englewood Cliffs, NJ: Prentice-Hall, 1995).

Donald E. Lundberg, *The Restaurant: From Concept to Operation,* 2nd ed. (New York: John Wiley & Sons, 2001).

Paul McVety, Sue Marshall, and Bradley J. Ware, *The Menu and the Cycle of Cost Control.* (Dubuque, IA: Kendall/Hunt Publishing Co., 1997).

Jack E. Miller and David V. Pavesic, *Menu Pricing and Strategy,* 4th ed. (New York: John Wiley & Sons, 1996).

Clement Ojugo, *Practical Food and Beverage Cost Control.* (Albany, NY: Delmar, 1999).

Nancy Scanlon, *Marketing by Menu,* 3rd ed. (New York: John Wiley & Sons, 1999).

Arno Schmidt, *Chef's Book of Formulas, Yields, and Sizes.* (New York: John Wiley & Sons, 1990).

Carl Scriven and James Stevens, *Food Equipment Facts.* (New York: John Wiley & Sons, 1982).

Albin G. Seaborg, *Menu Design Merchandising and Marketing,* 4th ed. (New York: John Wiley & Sons, 1991).

Frances Sizer and Eleanor Whitney, *Nutrition Concepts and Controversies,* 7th ed. (Belmont, CA: Wadsworth, 1997).

The Sourcebook of Zip Code Demographics, 10th ed. (New York: CACI Marketing Systems, 1995).

Tableservice Restaurant Trends. (Chicago: The National Restaurant Association Research Department 1988).

Peter E. VanKleek and Hubert E. Visick, *Menu Planning: A Blueprint for Profit.* (New York: McGraw-Hill, 1974).

Rande L. Wallace, *Introduction to Professional Foodservice.* (New York: John Wiley & Sons, 1996).

Index